BUSINESS CONCEPTS
AND MODELS

BUSINESS CONCEPTS AND MODELS

New Words for Old Ideas

Garth Holloway

Acknowledgements

With thanks to:
Shamim Ur Rashid for the cover design;
Victor-Adrain Cruceanu for the graphics;
Stephany Aulenback for editing the book;
Charles, Kailash, and Venkatesh for their friendship; and Russell Swanborough
for informing so much of my foundation thinking; and finally
Amit Kumar Das for his unbelievable inspiration.

Dedication

To my late father with all my love.

Contents

Organisational Culture..11

Understanding Information..24

Defining Business Requirements 41

Defining the Business Architecture...48

Policy and Rules: Similar But Different 66

Business Process Improvement and Performance Management............71

Customer Value Management 87

KPIs, SLAs and Other Measurements.......................................95

Governance 105

To Grow Shareholder Wealth 115

Managing Change..129

Preface

Thank you for taking the time to read some or all of the articles contained in this book.

This is the first in a series of three books. The second book is a collection of short articles on change management and the third provides a range tools and techniques for the manager's kitbag.

The purpose of the book is to consolidate and capture my thoughts and ideas across a wide selection of common business concepts that a manager may be expected to encounter throughout the various stages of their career.

The articles are not intended to provide detailed instructions or methodology on how to apply each concept. Rather the intent is to provide enough detail to convey the essence of the concepts, sufficient for the reader to apply them in their own business without the rigidity of an instruction manual.

As each paper is written as a stand-alone article, a number of the central concepts are repeated in the different papers. This has been kept to a minimum but could not be completely avoided.

Organisational Culture

Over the last 20 years or so, my consulting has broadly focused on performance improvement and business transformation. Having said that, it is also worth noting that for nearly all the clients I have worked with and for all the projects I have completed, the vast majority have benefited from an improvement in performance but very few clients have truly transformed themselves.

In my experience, business transformation cannot be achieved without a substantial challenge to the prevailing culture. But as with all improvement projects, to change the status quo requires that you understand what the status quo is. Or, in consulting speak, understand the "As Is" and then define and move to the "To Be."

Understanding the current culture in an organisation is readily achieved through the administration of a survey or organisational diagnostic tool. I have used a few and found that most of them use a foundation model against which the survey results are modelled.

For example, the Roger Harrison diagnostic identifies four organisation types: Power, Role, Achievement and Support. The diagnostic then indicates the appropriate type to describe your organisation.

There is nothing wrong with this approach. Having a foundation model is a good place to start, but it is important to validate that conceptually the model represents your organisation. If you disagree with the idea of restricting your organisation to Harrison's four types, then his diagnostic is not suitable for your company.

Executives know that the culture is in some way a reflection of them, and it is possible that they could reject any foundation model that doesn't broadly align to their view of the organisational culture, or what the culture should be. Using the Harrison example, a CEO may privately support a Power culture, but publically espouse a Support culture and therefore will not use the Harrison diagnostic as it may expose his private views.

There is no easy way to mitigate this besides helping executives accept that when it comes to the "As Is" there is no right or wrong answer. All modern diagnostics should broadly give you the same answer, and recognition and understanding is substantially more important than how the result is labelled.

Equally important is the level of detail provided. What you don't want is really fine detail as each person in the organisation will have their own interpretation of what the culture is and what it means to them. And an individual's interpretation of the culture is heavily influenced by their own personal circumstances and views on life. It is easy for a person to pick out the few aspects of the culture that support their behaviour and ignore the multitude of other cues that challenge it.

Given this, changing the culture at the individual level is a very long game and likely to yield a very poor result.

What is important is to fully understand how the perceived current culture is influencing the behaviour of *groups* of people, since different groups may have different interpretations of it.

Everyone considers themselves part of the business, but acts in accordance with their "local" culture. It is similar to there being different dialects of English between towns and villages. They all identify themselves as English, but at the detail level, they acknowledge and celebrate the differences.

The Internal and External Environments

For me, the two drivers of culture are the:

1. **Internal** environment and
2. **External** environment

While this may seem simplistic, it does get more complex as you examine the two environments.

The Internal Environment

The **internal** environment is the product of:

1. Leadership
2. Management style
3. Rewards

The prevailing organisational culture is the intersection of the four drivers:

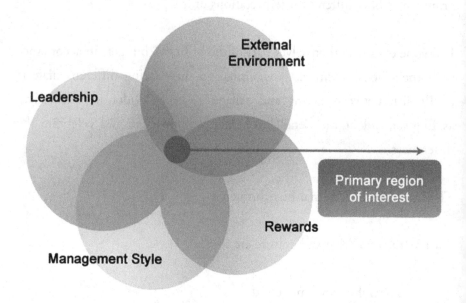

The *primary region of interest* represents the point at which the politics of the four drivers are most in harmony and this becomes the prevailing culture of the company.

Leadership and Management style is often the same thing at the CEO level. As soon as you move down the hierarchy they separate and leadership may become less of a factor, and management style can start to dominate.

The more senior the role, the greater the influence an individual's management style has on the culture of the company. It is not hard to accept that a supervisor may create a micro-culture within their area of control and that this would not have significant influence on the culture of the rest of the organisation.

On the other end of the spectrum, the management style of the senior executive of the company will have significant influence on the company culture. If their style is to be cautious and to enforce detailed analysis into the decision-making process, then this will create a very different culture to the company where the senior executive actively empowers and enables his managers and is willing to make decisions on 60% of the facts.

The influence of Leadership on the organisational culture is enormous. My view is that just because a company has a leader (Managing Director, CEO, Owner etc.), does not mean they have leadership. For me, leadership is the capability to engage the hearts and minds of people and cause them to emotionally invest and believe in a vision for the future.

Leadership can therefore manifest itself at any level in the organisation. The higher up the organisation, the more it will influence the culture. As a result you can have great managers who are poor leaders and vice versa. Depending on whether the CEO's strength is in leadership or management will significantly influence the culture of the organisation.

Reward

Reward is the third arm of the internal environment and I consider it to be as equally important as the management and leadership arms.

The salient point is that rewards refer to the *receipt* of the reward, not the *giving*. This means that for any given individual, rewards can be intrinsic and extrinsic.

Intrinsic reward is the reward that a person bestows on themselves for the job they are doing.

As a typical example, a charity worker is more likely to frame the work they do in a way that allows them to see themselves as giving back to society. If they were in it for the money then it is unlikely that they would last, as charities never have enough money and the motivation is wrong. Rather they need their internal reward system to provide the self-value needed to continue.

By comparison, a hard-nosed businessperson is less likely to rely on their internal reward system for recognition, choosing rather to measure themselves by the external rewards they receive for the work they do. In this case, reward = recognition and the most obvious examples are salary, car, office and title.

Consider the maxim: "Tell me how you are measured and I will show you how you behave." For the purposes of this paper I will take poetic licence and equate measure with reward: "Tell me how you are rewarded and I will show you how you behave." Behaviour and culture are inextricably linked.

The simple, earlier definition of company culture—the way we do things around here—can also be defined as "the way we behave as a company." If the reward is money and materialistic gain, then the culture will have an orientation of achievement and power. If the reward is self-fulfilment and non-materialistic gain, then the culture will orientate towards humanism and self-sacrifice.

The External Environment

The external environment is normally beyond the control of the company and its staff. There are a few cases such as Jack Welsh, Bill Gates, Steve Jobs etc., where the person has influenced the external environment.

The influence of the external environment is a product of the mix of global and local legislation, speed of transactions, size of transactions, average age of decision-makers, national identity and the social impact of getting it wrong.

To explain speed and size of transactions, consider a currency trader. They can place trades in billions of dollars and are "in and out" of the market in 20 minutes. Dealing with those sorts of sums has to distort the way the trader sees the world. A loss of $10 million is quickly shrugged off—it was only $10 million after all. To survive and flourish in this environment requires a very specific type of personality. My experience is that they work in a culture that encourages staff to play and work hard. Long hours in the pub are not unusual and to fit into the team a person would need to embrace this aspect of the corporate culture.

The national culture will have a strong effect on the organisational culture. To use a few stereotypes: Western culture is founded on freedoms, equality, and rights, particularly at the individual level. The national culture is generally one of success, and businesses are built in the same mould. The outlook tends to be financially driven and the short to medium-term is emphasised.

Eastern culture appears very different to me. There is an equal determination to be successful, but with a much stronger focus on the community and with deep respect for history. Profit is important but over the medium to long-term. Society's expectations of its citizens will have a substantial influence on how people think and behave at work and, by extension, a strong influence on the organisational culture of the businesses within that society.

The question now arises—how do you set or change the culture?

How to Set or Change Culture

Changing the organisational culture is exceptionally difficult as it requires changing behaviour.

Let's say the "As Is" survey has defined the current culture. The next step is to define the *desired* culture. How does the leader wish the company to behave? Closing the gap becomes the challenge.

Using the simple definition of culture—*the way we do things around here*—defining the desired culture obviously becomes—*the way **we want** to do things around here*. This can have many elements:

- **Time**—point of focus: past or present, short or mid-term
- **Communication**—formal or informal, high or low context
- **Space**—private or shared
- **Individualism**—recognition of individuals or teams
- **Competitiveness**—high or low
- **Structure**—flexible or ordered
- **Environment**—high or low control
- **Power**—equality or hierarchy orientated

This list is only an example. Each company should come up with their own list of drivers for their desired culture. A good place to start is any existing measures of the current culture. Determine what aspects of the existing organisational theatre, rituals and ceremonies are reinforcing the current culture and then consider how they could be challenged and reinterpreted.

It is however relevant to ask: should the company change the culture?

In certain organisations the culture is widely known and accepted—for example in the military, and the mines.

Both these working environments have a very strict culture of "do what you are told," as this culture is vital to the safety of the employee. For example I once witnessed a small underground rock fall. The rocks landed on a miner's ankles, breaking bones. The poor man was in a lot of pain and was taken away for medical assistance. Concurrently a charge sheet was written up against him as he should have made the working environment safe before entering. This work practice was not negotiable and his tardiness in this matter resulted in him having broken bones and a date with the in-house judiciary once he was out of hospital. I asked if the broken bones were enough punishment and was told—absolutely not. There is no room to question instructions given underground.

Google and Facebook are companies that appear to be on the other end of the spectrum. In each, the rules of the traditional working culture have been significantly challenged. From a theatre point of view, staff can dress largely as they please, workstations/work areas are less proletarian in their nature and layout. Creativity is strongly encouraged. As companies whose success relies on leading the market, they cannot afford to have a culture that inhibits creativity.

What Next?

Once the new culture is defined, all that you really have is a document describing an organisation that is similar but different to your current one. To implement this new culture and take it to a point where the employees use it to drive their behaviour takes substantial effort and frequently some very physical changes.

The easiest thing to physically change is the organisation chart. This may be as simple as title changes or as dramatic as changes to reporting lines. Each change sends a different message to the staff.

Another change that is equally dramatic—but takes slightly more effort—is changing the physical working environment.

One of my clients recently changed from a traditional workstation environment to an activity-based working environment where no one has a set desk, or telephone. There are no desktop computers and desks are tidied every night. Each person has a locker for their papers. The move was expensive but the message was blunt. We are going to do things differently from now on.

The initial change here was a dramatic change to the *theatre*. As a result, staff were forced to change their behaviours, and new ceremonies and rituals were introduced. Legacy behaviour from the previous work environment was seen to be obstructive. While my client did not necessarily set out to change the culture, they did achieve a positive change through a dramatic change to their theatre.

Change the People

The problem is that no matter how much you change the theatre in which the play is delivered, if you keep using the same actors, you may soon be getting the same performance quality as before.

A complex change is changing the actual staff members. I subscribe to the maxim—if you can't change the people, change the people. Moving a key person sideways or out of the organisation is a clear message of the intent to establish a new way of doing things. It also ensures that the company does not slide back to the old way of doing things.

While I agree that the company will always have an overarching culture, it is also expected that once the company has migrated to the new culture, each department will have its own interpretation of the new culture, based on the function of the department and the personality of the departmental manager.

Consider: the new company culture is to delight the customer and senior managers now dress in corporate casual and have increased expense accounts for customer lunches. This does not mean that the credit office should be any less aggressive in identifying potential bad debts.

Customer delight can never be their culture or mantra.

The same applies to an in-house quality assurance laboratory. For them it really doesn't matter what the culture is. They must test to specification and fail products that do not meet it. It can be argued that this is ensuring customer delight, even if it means upsetting the customer.

Company Language

One of the most difficult aspects of changing the organisational culture is changing the lexicon of the company.

Over time, the company builds up an internal vocabulary. The words people use provide direct insight into how they think. It is very difficult to convince anyone that the words you use do not reflect the way you think. Saying something once can be a joke. Repeated use of words just becomes the way you think. Racial statements are an easy example. Said once, it can be a joke in poor taste. Say it multiple times and you are a racist, even if you don't admit it to yourself.

Less easy examples are the use of words such as "customer" versus "client" or "locked in" contracts versus "termed" agreements. These words can mean the same thing but have different connotations. Using the right words and, importantly, no longer accepting words that do not reflect the new culture, is a significant step forward to embedding the new culture.

Companies should want to sign their customers up to a term contract—this provides certainty of cash flow. They shouldn't want to *lock* their clients in. It implies malice of forethought and behaviour. They don't want staff thinking of ways to lock clients in; they want staff thinking of products that can be sold on term agreements. The principles are the same, but the mental framework is different. Often the public face of the company will use language such as term contracts but privately they may discuss how they can launch products that will lock their customers in. To change the culture this private vocabulary must be stamped out.

To summarise: to change the way people think, get them to change the way they speak. Once they think differently, then they will behave differently and the new culture will embed itself.

It is quite likely that the staff will need some assurances that the new behaviour is acceptable. On this matter there is no better way for embedding the new culture than for the staff to see the senior executives exemplifying it. Staff will see it's acceptable and the new culture will start to take hold.

I will close with the note that cultural change is not for the fainthearted. It can take years to complete and if a company does not have the stomach for driving change over a long period, then it is probably better not to start. Giving up halfway means you will have a new culture, but you won't know what it is.

Understanding Information

This chapter comprises two parts. Initially it discusses and defines information from a theoretical point of view and then places the theory in a practical business context using three examples. By way of accreditation, my foundation thinking on this topic stems from conversations with, and the writings of, Russell Swanborough. He is most certainly a genius and a person who should be speaking on the world stage.

The essence of Swanborough's message is that there should be no such thing as an IT strategy. Rather there should be an "I and T" strategy or simply an "I" strategy on its own which is implemented through the application of "T."

The Information Technology (IT) world is, or close to, a trillion dollar industry and most of this money is spent on the purchase of technology. Significantly, the study of information is not common practice in the business world.

The separation of information from technology is mandatory in order to recognise information as something tangible in its own right. By definition once something is tangible it has attributes. To understand information is to understand its attributes.

What Is Information Made Up Of?

Information is made up from two primary attributes: **Quality** and the **Physical**.

The **quality** attribute comprises the following elements:

1. Relevance: Who need to produce or receive the information?
2. Accuracy, defined as a level of precision
3. Timeliness: When should the information be produced or received?
4. Support: How do you get help on the information?
5. Accessibility: How will the information be accessed?
6. Completeness: What information is required? (Typically this is the only attribute fully documented by a business analyst)

The primary principle behind these elements is that they are *intangible*. They don't really exist and if something does not exist it cannot be directly addressed, only indirectly.

The **physical** attribute comprises the following elements:

1. Collect: The manner by which information is collected.
2. Store: The manner by which information is stored.
3. Process: The manner by which information is processed.
4. Distribution: The manner by which information is distributed.

By contrast these elements are very *tangible* and can be addressed directly.

Consider the person who complains to the doctor that they have a headache, runny nose, dizziness and sore joints. The doctor listens to these symptoms and diagnoses a severe cold. He then asks what the patient has been doing to make him that sick. "Walking in the rain" is the reply, to which the doc replies, "Well, stop doing *that* and you won't get sick."

It is a classic case of cause and symptoms. You can't treat symptoms; you can treat the cause.

The same applies to information. The quality attributes are the symptoms and the physical attributes are the cause. You cannot change a quality attribute directly, only indirectly through the physical attributes.

Consider the manager who complains that the information they receive is inaccurate, late and lacks relevance. To address these weaknesses, the analyst will review how the information is produced to determine what is causing the information to be late, inaccurate and irrelevant and will make changes accordingly.

These changes will include changes to *what*, *when* and *how* information is collected, how it is processed and who it is distributed to. In other words, the changes will be applied to the physical attributes. By changing the physical attributes you change the quality attributes.

The business community is predominately concerned about the quality attributes. Managers do not really care how the information is collected, just that it is accurate, accessible and complete. The quality attributes provide the business requirements, and these can only be resolved by the physical attributes.

The role of IT is to administer the physical attributes to improve the way information is collected, stored, processed and distributed. Hardware and software are good for collecting, storing, processing and distributing information.

This dual focus is almost solely responsible for the traditional gulf between the business and the IT shop. The business asks, "Why don't you give me what I ask for?" IT responds, "Why don't you ask for what you want?"

The Relationship Between the Physical and Quality Attributes

There is a many-to-many relationship between the physical and quality attributes.

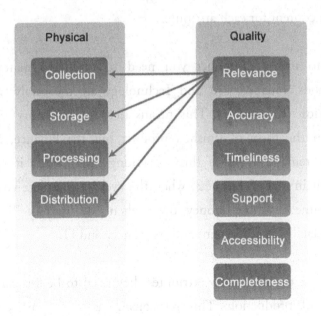

Source: Russell Swanborough

When an analyst is considering changing one or more of the quality attributes, they will need to consider how each physical attribute must be modified to effect the change. Equally, when changing a physical attribute, the analyst must consider the ripple effect on the quality attributes.

To extend these concepts it is important to describe what comprises the message or content that is moving between the physical and quality attributes.

Previously I mentioned that the business community focuses on the quality attributes. Therefore it is important to consider what makes up each attribute. The concepts of "relevance" or "accessibility" (and so on) are inconsequential in and of themselves. What makes them consequential is what content is presented for evaluation as relevant or accessible.

A business is made up of four elements or factors of production: Human Resources (HR), Inventory, Technology and Finance. These elements provide the content for each attribute.

Consider, to make a product you need to turn raw material into finished goods. Finance, HR and Technology are the catalysts for the transformation of inventory. This means that the inventory leaves the company in the form of finished product but the Finance, HR and Technology remain. I realise this is "a long bow" when it comes to Finance, but in a good business, when the cycle is complete you should have the same or more money than when you started. Technology includes all facilities, equipment and machinery and IT.

To understand the six quality attributes they need to be associated with the factors of production. This relationship is also a many-to-many relationship.

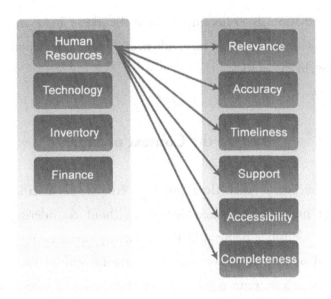

Each quality attribute is defined by its relationship to each factor of production. The quality attributes will always be applicable to every situation but it is acceptable that not every factor of production will be applicable to every situation.

By extension the relationship diagram now looks as follows:

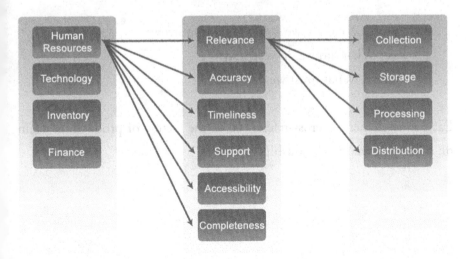

When information is collected, it must be done in a manner that considers its relevance to its audience. The same applies to all relationships in the model.

Adding the Context of Time

The key concept is that time provides context to decision-making. You cannot make an informed decision without considering the time component. Consider being told that a factory operates at 1000 units. Is that good or bad? Without time you have no way of knowing. One thousand units a minute is impressive; 1000 units a year less so. An investor offers to double your money. Do you invest? If the return is in a week, then it is a good deal; if the return is over 10 years then the value of the deal is diluted.

The relationship of time to information can become complicated.

In a pure sense there are three time domains.

1. Future: What are we going to do tomorrow?
2. Past: What did we do yesterday?
3. Present: What must we do today?

Each time element is cross-referenced to the factors of production, again on a many-to-many relationship.

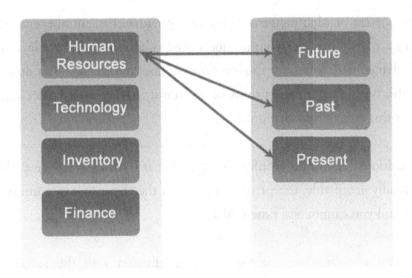

Traditionally these information relationships manifest themselves as lead or lag KPIs. Frequently, though, not all factors of production are measured. Often the primary focus is on finance and the other three factors are not really covered or ignored altogether.

For example: to understand Human Resources (staffing), it is important to define the future requirements for staffing, historical performance productivity, utilisation etc., and how staff are being allocated work packages on a daily basis. The same applies to all factors of production.

There is a fourth time component to information being the *absence* of time. The building blocks of a business are not associated with time, in that they do not change with the passage of time, or change so infrequently that the change is not material.

I term this forth component as data. It is descriptive in its nature. An example would be my name. You cannot add time to my name. Another example is the VIN number in a car. That never changes no matter who owns the car or what happens to the car over time. Part numbers do not change, nor do inventory bin numbers. The volume of inventory in a bin will change with time, but the bin number does not change. You do not use this type of information to make decisions; rather you make decisions about this type of information.

A traditional definition of information is that *it is data with context.* This is broadly acceptable, except that in terms of the above theory, context is time and you cannot add time to data.

I close this section on the theory of information with the following summary statements:

- Information can be defined as a time-bound package contextualised by its quality attributes.
- The value of information is determined by the adequacy with which the requirements of each quality component are met.

Types of Business Process

To extend the above concepts and place them in a business context requires the examination of process.

There are three types of process.

1. **Management** process, defined as operations management
2. **Business** process
3. **Information** process

The Information process is the glue that binds the Management process to the Business process.

The Management Process

A key part of a manager's role is decision-making, and effective decision-making is dependent on the quality of the information at hand. As mentioned earlier, the quality of information is determined by how well the requirements of each component of the quality attributes are met. The requirements are defined by what the manager needs to know about the factors of production at the time of decision-making. This creates the following:

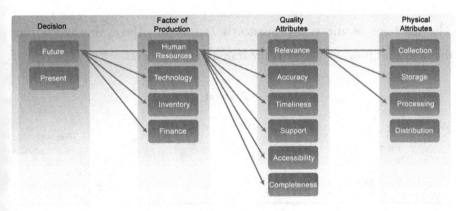

You can only make a decision about the present or the future. While doing so, you should consider the past—as often the pending decision will be to avoid the mistakes of the past. But you can't change the past. Therefore you can only make decisions for the present or future. To do this you need to know everything you can about the decision at hand, so all quality attributes must be addressed and you can only make a decision on the factors of production.

This statement holds true for strategic decision-making when the focus is on market share and corporate growth. In this case, completeness of information includes market data. But you make a decision on changing your presence in the market in order to affect the productivity of your factors of production—to improve the return on capital employed.

The Business Process

The business process refers to the transactional activities in a business. This can include processing applications in the back office or bending steel on the factory floor.

The marriage of the two processes is as follows. Above the line is the management process. Below is the transactional process.

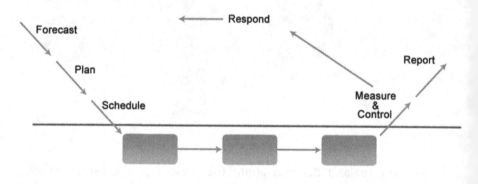

Source: Generic

Now, let's introduce the factors of production.

Inventory moves through the process and can be broadly defined. Inventory for the back office is bills, applications, invoices etc. Inventory for the production environment is raw materials, work in progress and finished goods.

Earlier I termed the other three factors of production as catalysts for change, in that they contribute to the transformation of inventory from raw material to finished goods without actually changing themselves. As previously mentioned, at times this can be a long bow when it comes to Finance.

It is valid at this point to separate IT out as distinct from production technology, as it provides the dual function of being a production engine for producing outputs such as forms and documents as well as being responsible for moving information along and between processes.

The picture now looks like this:

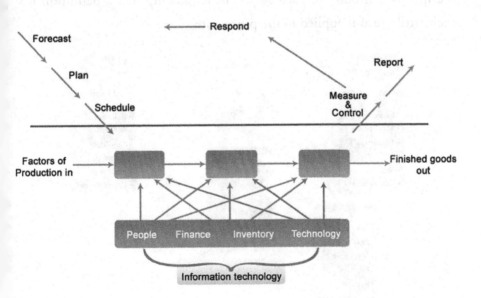

The left to right arrows represent the physical flow of goods and services. The remaining arrows are the flows of information. The diagram does not show it (to avoid becoming too cluttered) but there is an implied information flow from HR, Finance and Technology to all the elements of the Management process.

The following three case studies illustrate how these concepts can be used in a practical manner.

Case Study #1:

The client wished to prepare a business requirement to guide the purchase of a new ERP system.

We created a single high-level map of the business process and defined the quality attribute for each step. Then we completed a definition for each attribute as it applied to the process step.

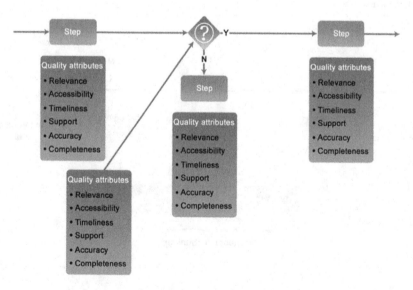

The following table is a very simplistic worked example of this concept.

Attribute Activity	Completeness	Timeliness	Accuracy	Support	Access	Relevance
Process step Example: Process subscriptions	• Member details • Name of bank • BSB • Account • Address • Subs amount • Payment schedule • Authorisation	• Subscriptions are processed on a monthly basis	• Financial figures to show 2 decimal points	•Membership system o Internal help desk • Banking system o Level 1 support from internal help desk o Level 2 support from bank help desk	• Remote Access • Desktop	• Finance • Divisional managers

Case Study #2:

A second example is where we used the attributes as the metrics in a diagnostic to determine the effectiveness of a recently implemented ERP system.

A survey focused on the business needs, not the technology itself. It set out to answer the question: is the business getting the information it needs to maintain maximum performance?

The survey separated the respondents into groups, those that create information (process performers) and those that receive it (managers). Process performers work in the business processes and are responsible for generating the information managers use in decision-making.

In the two example graphs below it is clear that process performers acknowledge there is a problem with the accuracy of their work, with a small number of respondents perceiving their output to be precise. Conversely, management perceives that the information they receive is moderately accurate at best.

Legend: Ct = Current, Id = Ideal.

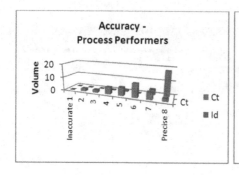

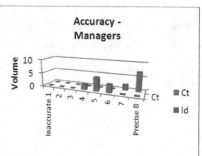

Similarly, process performers perceive that the work they produce tends towards being fully complete but managers perceive what they receive to be incomplete.

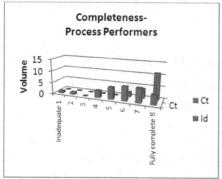

Case Study #3:

A third example is from a client who requested us to map the purchase-to-pay process, define the information requirements, define the system interface points and develop a business specification for an imaging and workflow solution.

As a first step we mapped the business process.

Then we determined the relevant information sets (e.g. supplier's invoice) required to manage the process and the information fields that make up each set.

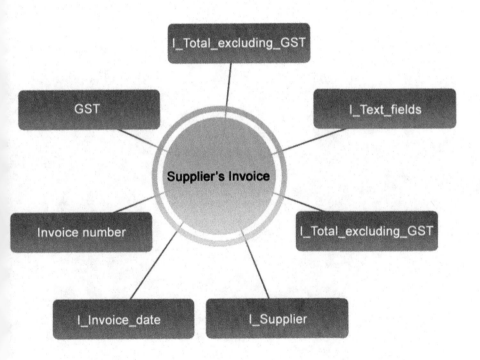

Then we determined the attributes of each field and its source. This detail is not shown due to confidentiality agreements.

Conclusion

I close with the observation that it will always be substantially more expensive to fix technology after its purchase than it would have cost to properly define the information requirements at the outset.

Defining Business Requirements

Contemporary business jargon has developed and grown to become the language of projects. Terms such as "facilitate," "functional," "change management," "process," "scalable," "seamless," "delight," "reengineer," "transformation," "value chain," etc. are now commonplace in project rooms and business documents.

Although these terms are widely used, their meanings are not universally understood. Consider the following:

When one person talks about change management, they might mean listening to the issues and ensuring they are communicated to senior project staff.

When another person talks of change management, they might be referring to taking the organisation on a journey of discovery—ensuring the staff understand why change is happening, that they feel included, heard and engaged in the project and that there is a formal organisation structure in place specifically set up to manage the change process.

Both definitions are right, and both have their place depending on the size and nature of the project and to whom you are talking.

So, imagine a business manager interviewing both consultants for a project. They might ask, "Do you have experience with change management?" Both truthfully say yes and both are right from their own perspective. But, without substantial digging, how does the manager draw a useable distinction between the two? It is probable the manager will use their own frame of reference to make the determination, thus introducing a third definition for change management.

The absence of a common vocabulary is most pronounced in workshops held to gather requirements. Those contributing to a project in the requirements gathering stage are frequently unknowingly unable to express their thoughts in a manner that ensures their intent is clearly heard and understood. When a participant says, "We must be able to recover a 98.5% yield from the de-boning process" is that a business requirement, functional requirement, capability statement or something else? How that statement is classified, depends on how much further information is gathered to support the requirement.

On the following page are my definitions for some of the commonly used terms. It is not important that you agree with my definitions, just that your project audience agrees with yours.

Goal	A qualitative statement.	I want to be rich.
Objectives	A quantitative statement. This is often the measure of the goal.	I want $10 million.
Capability	A statement of outputs. What process outputs are required to meet a business objective? 'What must we be capable of doing?'	The key takeout is that processes create or introduce organisational capability.
Functionality (Functional requirements)	This is the deliverable of technology into the business process. These requirements generally manifest themselves in the form of screens, forms and fields.	If it does not come from IT, then it is not functionality.
Non functional requirements	Everything that the process needs in order to create the required capabilities that is not delivered by IT.	This is a very broad concept and includes understanding and defining the requirements for people, finance and indirect technology needs. Capacity and competency are generally non functional requirements.
Rules	A rule is an absolute statement of documented company behaviour. A rule cannot be changed and does not have latitude. It can be repealed and reissued, but that is a different rule, not a changed rule.	i.e., Authority limits are rules. 'You cannot spend more than $50,000'. It is unambiguous.
Policy	Policies are statements describing your preferred behaviour in a given situation.	A credit officer can give credit if he/she believes the applicant to be honest and credit worthy. This then highlights that a rule and policy can conflict with each other and policy is administered within the boundaries of the rules.

Defining the Word "Requirement"

I have read many publications that define three levels of requirements:

1. Business requirements
2. Functional requirements
3. Technical requirements

I prefer to think of the term "business requirement" as the collective noun for goals and objectives, capability, competency and capacity, functional and non-functional requirements, rules and policy.

But I agree that there needs to be separation between these concepts, traditionally achieved as follows:

1. **Business requirements** tell us what we want to achieve.
2. **Functional requirements** tell us how it will be achieved.
3. **Technical requirements** are quite different and require specialist skills to prepare, and are written in such a way that a coder could read them and develop software accordingly.

The shortfall in the above is that there is another level of requirements—information requirements. The list should read:

1. **Business requirements**
2. **Functional requirements**
3. **Information requirements**
4. **Technical requirements**

Information requirements *glue* the technical requirements to the functional requirements. This requirement comprises screen and field definitions and attributes which are, in practice, the physical manifestations of the functional requirements.

Separating the elements you get the following.

Business requirements	Goal statements Objective statements Capability statements Capacity statements Competency statements Policy statements
Functional requirements	Functionality statements Non functional statements Rules
Information requirements	Screens and forms (information sets) Fields
Technical requirements	The physical interaction of the information requirements to each other. How technology will store, collect, process and distribute information.

We can then put it all together in a simple graphic:

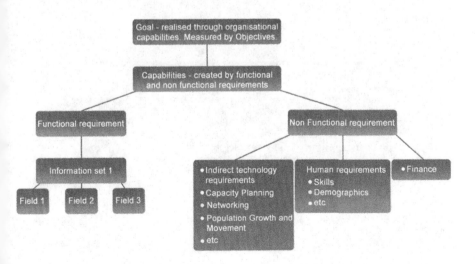

The above is a basic traceability model. Correctly constructed, it links business objectives to information fields, skills and finance.

So far I have not referred to business process. A process provides context for the requirements. It is not a requirement itself. It represents the preferred sequence for the functional requirements to manifest themselves to maximise business efficiency.

An individual process is the aggregation of some of the requirements. By extension, all processes should be the sum of all requirements for all capabilities. However it is not unusual to have processes that do not contribute to a capability and, conversely, capabilities without having a process to deliver them.

Introducing business process to the graphic you get:

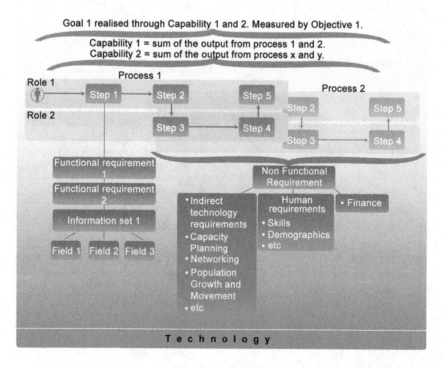

I close with the following observations:

- Functional requirements are generally associated with a process step. If you write up a functional requirement for a process you are in danger of describing a capability rather a functional requirement. This is a rule of thumb. Common sense should prevail.

- Non-functional requirements for human resources are generally associated with an individual (entire) process, and financial and indirect technical requirements would generally be associated with a group of processes.

- It is often very difficult to adequately classify a requirement—is it a capability, rule, functional requirement and so on? My definitions are a good guide, and if you classify most requirements correctly, then the remaining incorrect classifications are probably of little consequence. The important thing is that the requirement was noted in the first place.

- Technology spans all processes. You define functional requirements for a specific process/process step, but you implement technology for multiple processes. The technology is the aggregation of all the requirements.

- Business process reengineering projects spend huge amounts of time and money defining future state processes and comparatively little effort on functional and information requirements and almost no effort on non-functional requirements. Then they question why the project is not delivering the benefits promised in the business case.

Defining the Business Architecture

My preferred business architecture model is shown in the schematic. The model reinforces that people/process/technology are intertwined and it is impossible to develop a true understanding of any individual element in the model in isolation of the context provided by at least one of the other nine points.

This chapter focuses on the three primary elements of people, process and technology.

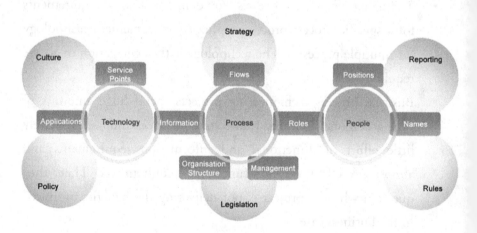

The remaining business concepts such as culture, rules etc., will be addressed in separate documents.

Each of the three elements is summarised below and then discussed in more detail.

People

There are three elements:

1. **Names**: refers to specific individuals. It is the names of employees, suppliers and/or partners in the extended architecture.
2. **Positions**: refers to the formal position the individual holds in the business.
3. **Roles**: refers to the role(s) the position can fill in the day-to-day operations on the business.

Process

There are three elements:

1. **Flows**: refers to the transactional flow of activity within the business. Typically these flows are called process maps, but for a business architecture model this term is too generic, as there are two other processes that need to be described as part of the architecture. The transactional flow is a better term. This is process 1 of 3.
2. **Management**: refers to the active management of a specific process. In this case management is a defined process (process 2 of 3) and comprises specific steps as shown:

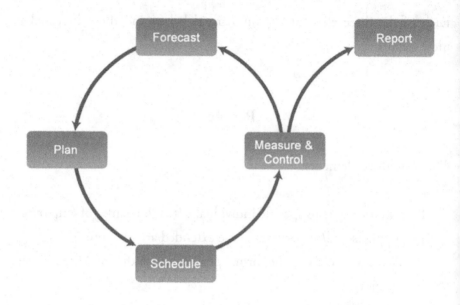

Source: Proudfoot PLc

3. **Organisational structure**: refers to the aggregation of the individual management processes to form the organisational structure.

Technology

There are three elements:

1. **Service Points**: refers to those points in the process where information needs to present itself.
2. **Information**: refers to the specific information or information set that must be presented at the service point. This is process 3 of 3.
3. **Applications**: refers to the specific application or application sets that will provide the information.

People

The most basic element here is the people themselves, the employees. They can be represented by a list of names on a page. By itself, this is just a list and of limited value. When associated with positions and/or roles its value increases significantly. This relationship is typically established with a **RACI** table. A **RACI** table describes who is **R**esponsible, **A**ccountable, **C**ontributes, and is **I**nformed by the process.

Process / Role	Accounts Payable	Approver	Bank	Cheque Signatories	Corporate Finance Manage
Accounts Payable					
•Generate Vendor AP report on inactive vendors	R				
•Inactive vendors with no activity in last 12 months	R				
End	R			R	R
•Generate Vendor AP report	R				
•Check vendor against Vendor AP report	R				
•Ask requester to complete a vendor setup form	R				
•Complete a vendor request form					
•Update vendor details	R				
•Scan invoice	R				
•Save on F Drive	R				
•Notify of updates required	R				I
•Receive request email and activate vendor					R
•Notify all of completed activation	CI				R
Process AMEX invoices and staff expenses		A			
•Reminders sent with deadlines for submissions	R				
•Download AMEX transaction statement					
•Attach receipts and statements					
•Update Expenses template					
•Send to Approver		I			
•Code and approve		R			
•Invoices approved		R			

In the matrix, column A represents all the processes that make up the accounts payable function and the process steps of each process. This is the basic building block for job descriptions, training materials, user access security models etc.

A key consideration when using this approach is to decide upfront if you will use job titles/positions, or role descriptions as you map the processes. This distinction is important, as staff will frequently perform a role that is not traditionally associated with their position or title. Often this is the case when managers intermittently stop *managing* the process and start *working in* the process. For example: a finance manager may decide to perform an invoice run or pay a supplier. Both of these actions would normally be completed by an accounts receivable or payable clerk. When the manager performs these tasks, then they are taking on the role of the clerk.

In some cases there is no issue; in other cases the manager may not have the authority to access the system as they may also inadvertently receive the means to see privileged information such as the payroll. Therefore best practice is to map the business using roles, and then determine which position is entitled to play which role.

An alternate view is a comprehensive job description that relates the role to specific processes and process steps. This will substantially assist training and recruitment. The following is a simple example of such a job description and could include:

Description of role	The Role will ensure the timely update of leasing records and databases, processing of rent roll changes and the collaborative management of arrears.
Role type	Person
Represented in these diagrams	1.1 Allocate receipts against outstanding invoices 2.1 Capital transaction fees 3.1 Convert agreements to lease 4.1 Lease renewal or option 5.1 Leasing fees 6.1 Maintain periodic rent roll 7.1 Manage adjustments to CAPEX project budget
Responsible for these process steps	**Capital transaction fees** • ....on whether the approved fee has changed • Calculate ...... or adjusted fee based on sales value • Forward to analyses for verification amount and charging entities • Forward .... for approval • Forward to Cap .... Mgr for approval • .... AR to .... invoice **Leasing fees** • Send to portfolio .... for approval • Check fee calculation and confirm • Calculation correct • Update leasing fee overview per hand • Update .... overview • Sent overview to analytics team • Instruct AR team
Consulted at these process steps	Manage .... • Review .... report
Informed by these process steps	Capital transaction fees • Calculate new or adjusted fee based on sales value • .... • Review and add comment

Process

Understanding business process starts with establishing the hierarchy of processes. Decomposing the business from a macro enterprise process view to a detailed process view is fundamental to understanding "lines of business," silos and the "hand-off" between processes.

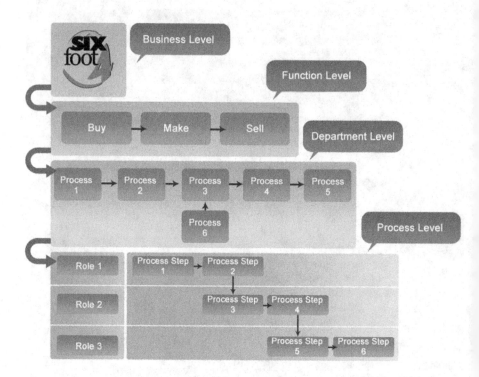

Traditionally business analysts will talk of process level "X," where X is normally 1 to 5. Detailed process flows are typically level 4 and procedures or work instructions are level 5. Levels 1 to 3 represent how the business aggregates the detailed processes into functions and departments.

When mapping a business or transactional process there are a few guidelines that can improve the quality of the activity:

Use a consistent template. If you map one process using the swim lane format, then map all processes the same way. Experience shows that business analysts tend to prefer the swim lane layout and end users and trainees prefer role-based process flows.

Swim lane layout	Role based layout

- Use **roles not positions** wherever possible.
- Describe the process step using a **verb-noun combination**. Always try to start the process step description with a verb.
- There are **three types of automation**: manual processing, computer-assisted manual and fully automated. Only fully automated steps should receive their own swim lane if your methodology is to show technology as a role. Computer-assisted manual should be shown as part of the process step.
- A process map should be **8 to 12 steps**.
- Keep system process maps **related but separate** from business process maps.
- Define the **trigger process(es)** and the **hand-over process(es)**.
- Ensure you keep the **unit of measure (UOM)** in mind at all times. The UOM is what triggers a process. For example, a UOM is an application form. This will be particularly important when

the time comes to calculate process volumes, standard costs and staffing needs.

- **Identify any reports** produced.
- **Identify all control points** in the process. There may be different control points for different compliance needs in the business.

Management Process

The management process is a separate process from the transactional process. The management process is represented by the collection of control documents the manager uses to control the processes in their portfolio. The term "manager" includes everyone from Team Leader to Chief Executive Officer. Control documents include everything from white boards on the wall, clip boards, volume counts, electronic light boards, to detailed printouts from the ERP system.

The fundamental principle is that these documents represent the controls the manager uses to work "on" the process, not "in" the process.

The management process has two halves.

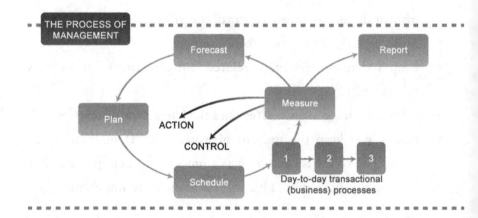

The transactional process separates the two halves of the management process.

The first half comprises those controls that manage demand for the process. They tell the manager the hourly/daily/weekly/monthly etc. volume for the process and the resource requirements needed to meet that volume.

The second half comprises the control documents that the manager uses to measure and control the process through KPIs etc.

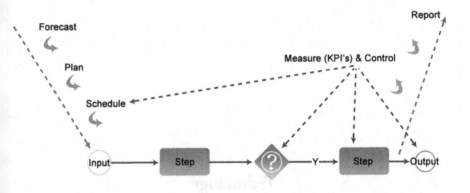

The following schematic is an illustration of a simple scorecard in MS Excel:

Manager											Year	2012	
											Month		
						Actuals					Cumulative		
KPA	KPI	UOM	Freq	Planned	Week1	Week2	Week3	Week4	Week5	Planned	Actual	Variance
Department/Division/Org Unit — Performance	KPA 1	Metric 1	Hr	W									
		Metric 2	Hr	W									
		Metric 3	Hr	W									
	KPA 2	Metric 4	#	W									
		Metric 5	$	W									
		Metric 6	#	W									
		Metric 7	$	W									
		Metric 8	#	W									
		Metric 9	%	W									
		Metric 10	#	W									
	KPA 3	Metric 11	#	W									
		Metric 12	$										
		Metric 13	#	W									
		Metric 14	$										
		Metric 15	#	W									
		Metric 16	$	W									
Compliance	Control type	Metric 17	#	W									
	Control type	Metric 18	Hrs	W									
		Metric 19	#	W									

Each process has its management. This is founded on the principle that you can have process without management, but you cannot have management without process.

As many management processes are combined, so is the organisation structure established.

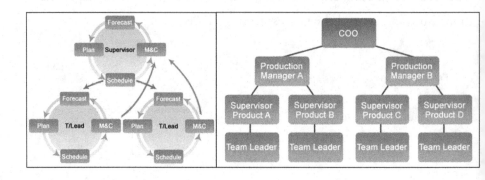

Technology

The third major element is technology. And the key sub element is information, as it is information that glues the business together.

There are two types of information. Information *within a process* and information used to *manage the process*.

When modelling information, it is important to take into account the attributes and characteristics of information. Of particular relevance are the physical and quality attributes of information as they define what information will be presented at a service or control point and how it will be presented.

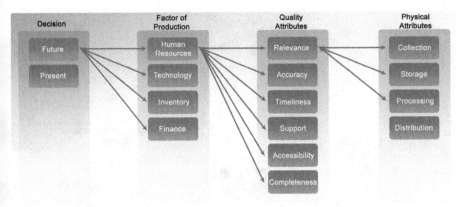

Defining each attribute requires that the information architect consider information sets and fields. Many fields make up a set. An example of a field is First Name. Surname would be a different field. Grouping common or related fields creates a set. A set can be what is displayed on a screen, a report or a printed document. The boundaries of a set are defined by the quality attributes.

Once the architect has defined what information is required and where, then they can model how the information will be gathered by defining the detail behind the physical attributes.

The following is a simple example of how this can manifest itself. The report represents the information set. The fields are shown as are their source application.

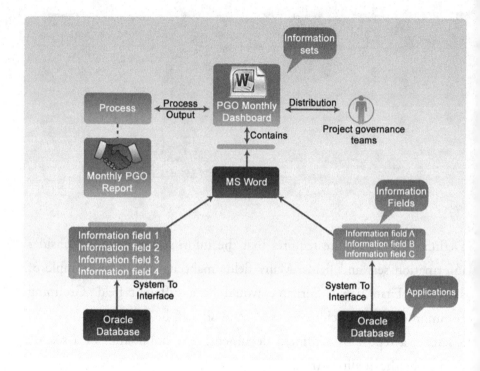

An alternative view of information sets and fields could look as follows. In either view, the attributes of both the sets and the fields would require further definition—for example, the alphanumeric, decimal places, arrays, etc.

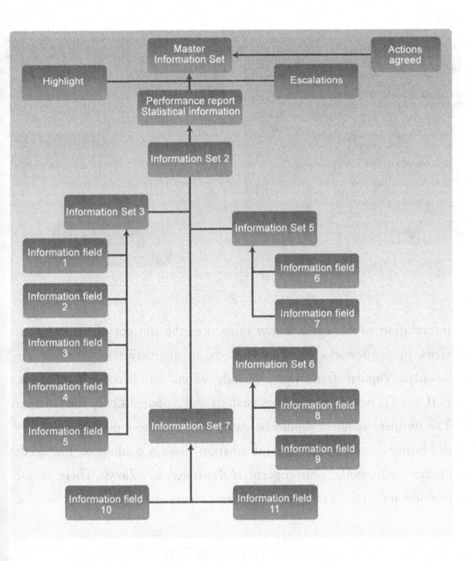

Information *within a process* can also be readily summarised in a matrix that aligns the information requirements, in the form of rules or functionality sets, to the business processes.

Accounts Payable	Accounts Payable	Approver	Bank	Cheque Signatories	Corporate Finance Manage
• Generate Vendor AP report on inactive vendors		Column = Transactional processes			
• Inactive vendors with no activity in last 12 months					
End	X			x	x
• Generate Vendor AP report	-				
• Check vendor against Vendor AP report	X				
• Ask requester to complete a vendor setup form	X				
• Complete a vendor request form					
• Update vendor details	X			ROW view - These are the rules sets.	
• Scan invoice	X			How the individual	
• Save on F Drive	-			rules are grouped	
• Notify of updates required	X				
• Receive request email and activate vendor					x
• Notify all of completed activation	X				x
Process AMEX invoices and staff expenses		X			
• Reminders sent with deadlines for submissions	X				
• Download AM...	Rows - The list of all				
• Attach receipt	rules governing the			The same applies to	
• Update Expen	system			functionality and functionality	
• Send to Approver			X	sets, or system and system	
• Code and approve			X	sets	
• Invoices approved			X		

Information to *manage a process* introduces the concept of management views or frameworks. A framework is an alternative way to see the business. Popular frameworks include eTom for Telecommunications, ITIL for IT, APQC for business analysts and Sarbanes Oxley for Finance. The business architect should be aware of the frameworks being used by the business, and model the information flows according to the needs of each framework. This concept is illustrated as follows. There is one business and in this example, four different ways of looking at the business.

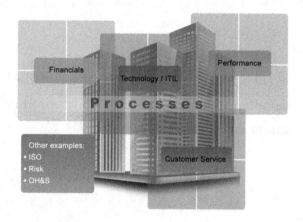

These views do not corrupt the message. Rather they focus it to remove "noise" and other irrelevant data. Frameworks guide the manager as to what should be considered when transacting the business process, and which parts of the process need to be controlled to ensure that the business is adhering to its internal policies and applicable external regulations, legislations etc.

Frequently the same process step is a control point for different frameworks.

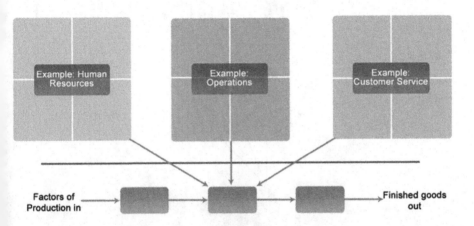

The difference is that each framework demands different information from the process step according to the risk being managed. When this is aligned to roles the extended model looks as follows:

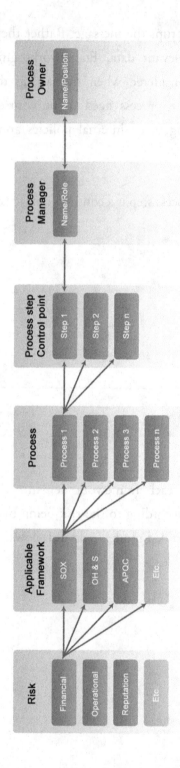

In summary, the relationship between the Management, Transactional and Information processes is depicted as follows:

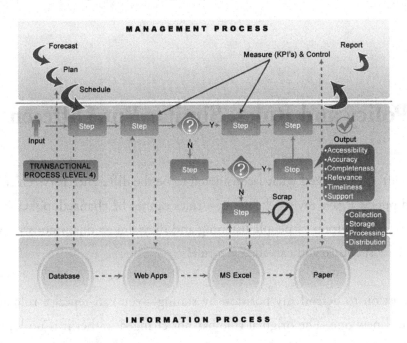

These three processes need to be treated as separate but related processes, and whether they are defined or not, all three will always exist.

Policy and Rules: Similar But Different

Recently I was asked what I considered to be the difference between rules and policy. I gave my stock answer—rules cannot be changed, policy can. There was a group of people listening and they almost unanimously said, "What, of course you can change a rule!"

I went on to defend my position by stating—you can repeal a rule and issue a new one. The original rule has not changed; rather it is no longer in force. A new rule has been issued and it is separate from the previous rule. Conceivably the original rule can still be reissued and both rules will be in force at the same time.

Policies by contrast can be changed and the "edges" of policy are not as defined as a rule.

Policy and rules are similar in that they both set out to guide behaviour. They differ to the extent that they allow the individual to make the final decision as to how they will behave.

The key attribute of a rule is that it must be precise. You are either complying with it or not. Consider the rule that you must stop at a red traffic light. There is nothing ambiguous about this rule. You either stopped or you didn't. You are not allowed to interpret the rule. When the fire alarm sounds above your desk, you do not get to decide whether you leave or not; you get up and go. (I admit that when it comes to fire drills, I frequently break this rule.)

Policy is often written up in an equally prescriptive manner. Most companies have a policy on bribes along the lines of: no employee will accept or offer a bribe. This statement is as prescriptive as a rule. In fact I would call it a rule that is frequently called a policy.

Policy sets the parameters that define how you will behave in a given situation. An example: staff is permitted to dress in business casual on Fridays. This policy does not explicitly define what business casual is, leaving it up to the individual to decide what is appropriate. A further example is: sales managers may spend $XX a month on business expenses. The policy does not define how the allowance should be spent, or on what.

In both examples, it is assumed that the individual will do the right thing and will behave in accordance with the values and objectives of the company. With rules, this freedom is removed and an individual's behaviour is prescribed.

This distinction is important when establishing organisational procedures. A procedure tells you how to do something. Typically a policy covers the entire procedure and provides the parameters of permissible decisions on what's appropriate behaviour when executing the procedure. Rules generally apply to specific tasks within the procedure and cannot be interpreted.

Despite the implication of the oft-used phrase "policies and procedures" both policy and rules exist separately from procedures and have a one-to-many relationship with procedures. This means that individual policies and rules can be associated with multiple procedures and procedural steps respectively.

Establishing rules is reasonably straightforward as the language of rules is "native" to managers. We are all comfortable expressing constraints on behaviour in terms of single statements. "You will . . ."; "You must . . ."; "You cannot . . .". Even when we intend to establish policy statements we typically express them as rules.

There is no easy methodology for establishing policy. As a guideline, the role of policy is to:

- translate values into operations
- reinforce compliance with legal and statutory responsibilities
- set standards, and
- improve the management of risk

A good place to start is with rules. Write down the rules that will apply to the area you wish to establish policy for. Then bundle similar rules into groups. These rules become the parameters of the policy statement. Read each rule in a group and write a business statement that covers all the rules in that group. This is your policy statement. Given that the statement is trying to cover all the rules in the group, it will by necessity, be appropriately vague.

Another method is to take a specific problem area in the business that you wish to manage with improved policy and establish a table that aligns policy with procedures and rules. Having these three items in one table quickly surfaces issues where policy is written as a rule and rules as policy.

As an example, the business issue addressed by the table is to reduce the risk of poor decision-making on tender submissions.

Policy	Procedure	Rule/s	Consequence
Decisions should be made from accurate information only and with visibility of known inaccuracies or estimates	• Preparers to clearly highlight estimates • The preparer must further highlight any estimates greater than [amount] • Inaccurate information is identified before decisions are made • Information must be reviewed by [who] before submission to [whom] • Bid information is verified by project manager before submission to [whom]	• Information is inaccurate if it contains an error in excess of $10,000 • Information is inaccurate if it is more than 1 week old • Any known or expected material changes [in excess of $10,000] must be adjusted before submission	If information is found to be innacurate, then the entire submission should be returned to the author for correction before a decision can be taken
Decisions should be made from complete information only	• The preparer will complete all mandatory headers and add additional information as required • The project manager reviews all information before submission to [whom]	• Missing artefacts must be highlighted on submission • Information is incomplete if any of the mandatory headers are not completed	Executive should reject incomplete submissions

The first policy statement uses the word "accurate." This is a relative term. The rules define how accuracy should be interpreted.

The second policy statement uses the word "complete." This is also a relative term. The rules define how completeness should be interpreted.

Completing the table should deliver relevant and useful policy statements.

In closing, I will say the real difficulty is managing the policies and rules once they are published. The last column in the table is "consequence." When it comes to rules and policies, if you are not prepared to manage them, do not bother establishing them.

Business Process Improvement and Performance Management

Business process improvement? The problem as I see it is that, generally, there is no such thing as a business process. When you map a process, you have just that, a process map. It is a piece of paper or screen view of what happens in the business. It is a graphical representation of routine, of behaviour, of what people do on a daily basis to turn inputs into outputs.

The issue here is—if processes don't exist, how do you make them better?

An easier question is—what does exist? The answer is "routines and habits." People come to work and complete their daily tasks using the same routine, day after day. The routine (processing sequence) is almost ingrained in them. They do not need to refer to operating manuals or ask colleagues for help. They know what to do—and when to do it. This routine is their daily habit.

(I do acknowledge that Business Process Management (BPM) solutions substantially automate processes and remove the reliance on habit and routine.)

A wise man (either Steve Rigby or David Lipschitz; they are both wise) once gave me the phrase: "Tell me how you are measured and I will show you how you behave." This phrase is brilliant as it unlocks the difficulties associated with business process reengineering. If you redefine process from being "a sequence of tasks completed in a sequential manner" to "a sequence of habits completed in a routine manner," then you have the answer. Change the habits to change the process.

So, how do you change a habit? You change the measures. Tell me how you are measured and I will show you how you behave. Change the measures = change the behaviours = change the habits = change the process.

I am not so one-eyed as to believe that measurement is the cure to all things process, but I am a firm believer in the idea that if you can't measure it, you can't manage it. So measurement is a good start when it comes to changing the process.

Minimise Decision-Making to Improve the Process

Many of you will be thinking that your process measures (KPIs) are reasonable and there is no need to change them. This is probably correct. The answer is to extend them, either on the same score sheet or in another sheet. Include measures of the specific points in the process where the process needs redefining (i.e. where bad habits occur).

Often, these points are not process-related at all. Rather, they are decision points within the process—points in the process where the worker has to make a call on the best way forward, where they have to break routine.

This can be for a multitude of reasons: not receiving all the information they need, the customer asking for something out of the ordinary, the computers are down, there is scheduled maintenance on a needed piece of machinery, etc.

Decisions cost money, increase headcount requirements, decrease the predictability of the process outcome and impact gross margins. To reengineer a process is to *minimise* decision-making in the process.

A process is never a single entity—rather it is a collection of paths. Each path is created by a decision.

Consider a decision with a 60/40 split. Immediately you have two paths, each carrying a different volume. One has 60% of the volume, the other has 40%.

Now imagine that the 40% path has a decision with a 70/30 split. Now there are three paths, with one carrying 30% of 40%. Not much volume at all. Every decision introduces another path.

Here is how those paths might look:

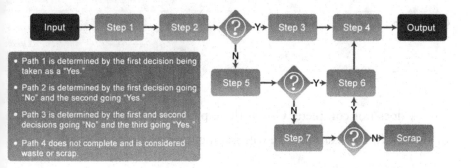

Paths 1, 2 and 3 all complete—they all end with a common output.

Path 1

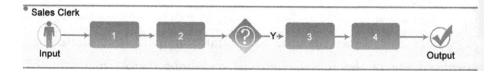

Path 2

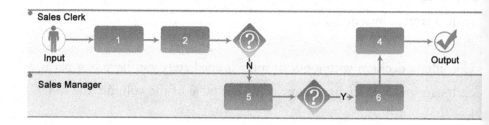

Path 3

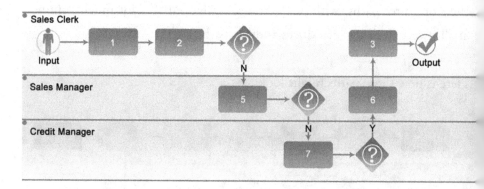

Path 4 does not complete. Often, these paths will be modelled as rework or similar. In this example, we will assume it simply leads to scrap.

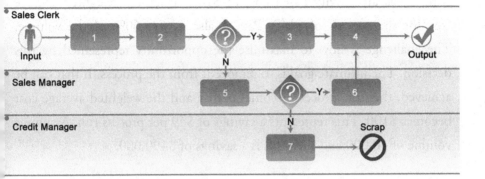

Once the process is mapped with the decision splits in place, the next piece of data to consider is the work and cycle time associated with each step or collection of steps. For example, step 1 takes 30 minutes to complete; the hand-off between steps 2 and 5 has a built-in four hour delay. So you plug in all this data. Then you need to attribute role costs to each step in the process.

Now you multiply volume x effort x cost. This will give you a weighted average of each path in the process.

Path	% of Volume in Path	Activity Based Cost	Weighted Average Cost
1	60	$100	$60
2	20	$200	$40
3	15	$300	$45
4	5	$80	$4
		Total	$149

Path 1 has an activity based cost of $100 versus the weighted average cost for the process of $149. Path 1 also carries 60% of the volume. The challenge is now to maximise the opportunity represented by this decision. The ultimate goal is to remove it from the process. If that can be achieved, then the process becomes path 1 and the weighted average cost becomes $100. This represents a savings of $49 per process run. Assume a volume of 10,000 and then this is a savings of $490,000.

The savings by process can be aggregated by department or function.

	The number of variations by which a single item could be processed		The working hours expressed in minutes		The average unit cost		The annual transaction cost for the process

| | | Unit Time | | | | Annual | | | |
Process by Function	Paths	Work (h)	Elapsed (m)	(d)	Unit$	Vol.	C..	FTE	Cost%
BUY									
PURCHASING	14	3.2	194	0.5	$144	3.936	$449,806	7.31	18%
RECEIPTS	28	0.4	26	0.5	$7.79	30,00	$233,700	7.47	9%
ACCOUNTS PAYABLE	63	0.6	35	1.0	$56	2,400	$134,520	0.81	5%
MAKE									
PICKING	18	1.1	68	2.0	$31	8,000	$246,560	5.20	10%
ASSEMBLY	102	1.8	105	2.3	$112	850	$95,591	0.86	4%
DISTRIBUTION	8	1.6	96	4.4	$361	895	$323,096	0.82	13%
INVOICE PROCESSING	17	0.3	15	0.4	$6.57	37,000	$243,090	5.44	10%
SELL									
CATALOGUES	14	25.0	1500	10.0	$51	6	$305	0.09	0%
MARKETING	3	6.0	360	30.0	$18.99	1,000	$18,990	3.45	1%
INVOICE PROCESSING	7	0.5	30	1.0	$18	100	$1,717	0.03	0%
IT MANAGEMENT									
USER ACCESS CONTROL	12	0.3	15	4.0	$7.80	25,000	$195,000	3.59	8%
ENQUIRY MANAGEMENT	11	0.9	56	0.2	$53	1,936	$102,724	1.04	4%
NEW USER SETUP	18	0.5	30	4.0	$20	21,600	$437,832	6.21	18%
					P%	00%	$2,482,990	42.30	100%
					factor	..%	$2,921,165	50	

Elapsed times are very conservative. Lower end estimates have been used throughout.

The average days elapsed to process a volume of 1 (drives customer service)	The annual transaction volume through this process	The full time equivalent staff requirement

There is a corresponding impact on staffing.

FTE By Internal Role - Current Mode of Operation													
Process	Role 1	Role 2	Role 3	Role 4	Role 5	Role 6	Role 7	Role 8	Role 9	Role 10	Role 11	Role 12	Total FTE
Buy													
Purchasing		2.0			1.3	2.9	0.70	0.330					7.26
Receipts					2.00	4.0	0.16		1.00	0.300			7.46
Accounts payable				0.5			0.3						0.77
Make													
Picking					1.7		2.0		0.6				5.17
Assembly													0.85
Distribution									0.8				0.82
Invoice Processing						0.6				4.0	0.4	0.4	5.40
Sell													
Catalogues		0.1											0.09
Marketing	1.4	2.0											3.40
Invoice processing				0.1		0.2							0.34
IT management													
User Access Control		3.6											3.57
Enquiry management		1.0											1.03
New user setup		6.2											6.17
	1.4	12.8	2.1	0.6	1.7	5.0	9.2	0.86	1.8	5.0	0.7	0.4	42.3

To get rid of the decision is to take the decision before the process starts. This can be achieved with process reengineering, policy or behavioural changes, or it can be forced with technologies such as imaging or workflow.

The following is an example of how a policy can be associated with a process and, by extension, the roles impacted by that policy.

Policy	Context	Impacted Roles
Example	Prepare valuation aggregation model	Financial Services PM Group Treasury Manager Senior Property Accountant Valuations and Investment Executive

Performance Management

Performance is best described as plan versus actual. What I set out to achieve versus what I did achieve. This is a simple concept and I have never quite managed to get my head around why companies don't do this well, especially as there is a huge industry selling business intelligence software that purports to do exactly this.

My experience has shown that supervisors are not taught to supervise. Let me explain.

The process of management is the same for all companies. Schematically, it looks like this.

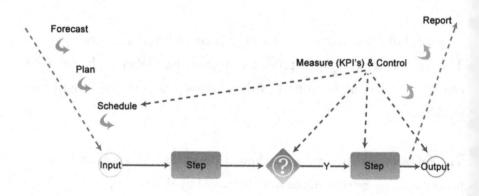

While the management process is common for all companies, the business process obviously differs by process and by company. Performance management links the two processes together.

First, as described above, you need to calculate the weighted average effort required to complete an iteration of the process. For example, to complete an invoice payment takes me 25 minutes. You can calculate this figure or you can guess it. One is more accurate than the other, but the main thing is to have consensus on the number.

Then (simplistically speaking) you multiply this number by the annual volume i.e. 10,000 invoices. Then divide the total by work hours and you have your Full-Time Equivalent headcount. In this case it will take one person 555 days, working 7.5hrs a day to complete the work. Or more rationally it will take 2.5 full-time staff to manage the volume.

Now you have your staffing level. The next step is to allocate them to work. They should be working at the standard of one invoice every 25 minutes. This assumes a constant flow of invoices.

In the management process, the step for allocating work is "schedule." This is a vital step in effective management and is the primary responsibility of the supervisor or team leader as it is directly responsible for managing cost.

Once the process has completed, it is measured. This should simply be a comparison of plan versus actual and the manager/supervisor will deal with the variance. Variances can be caused by poor process, low skills, laziness, pacing and a range of other issues. It is quite fascinating how many businesses miss this step. They have scorecards that measure "actuals," but seldom do they compare these *actuals* to the *plan*. You need to ask yourself: why bother measuring actuals if you are not comparing them to what you set out to achieve?

While it is important to measure specific transactions, it is equally important to use ratios to cross-reference transactional measures against each other to drive further insights. For example, the sales measure is going up—that is good. Costs are going up—that is not so good, but easily explained. But an analysis of the gross margin (GM) ratio may show that the GM percentage is declining sharply. That is terrible. It is only once you compare sales to costs do you get the true impact of the trends of the individual measures.

While the above is reasonably obvious, it is quickly forgotten that you can't fix a ratio. You can only fix the individual measures that make up the ratio—hence the need to manage the individual transactional lines.

Short Interval Control (SIC)

A key question is—how does the supervisor manage the individual measures in a way that any surprises are avoided and variances to plan are minimised? The answer is "Short Interval Control."

Short Interval Control (SIC) is the primary weapon in the supervisor's kitbag. It is broadly defined as "measuring the process at an interval that allows the supervisor to take action on an operational variance, before the variance causes customer promises to be broken and/or increased operational costs."

Consider a supervisor working the floor of a bottling plant. Bottles are whizzing around at a rate of hundreds or thousands a minute. Short interval control requires the supervisor to be checking his schedule every 15 minutes. If he waits an hour, the magnitude of scrap from a processing error would be enormous. Contrast this to a claims processing department. Each claim may take 90 minutes to complete. Short interval control may only require checks at two-hourly intervals.

This principle is illustrated in the following graphic:

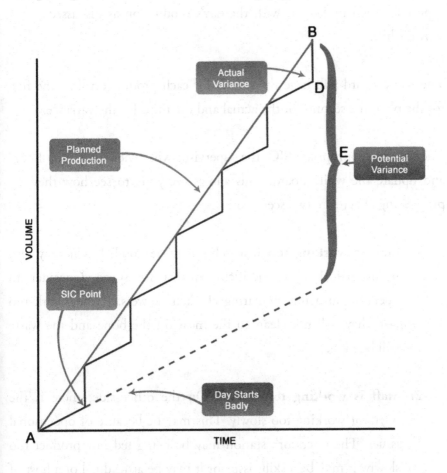

The day starts at point A. This should manifest as a start of shift meeting. At this time, the supervisor or team leader reviews the day's production targets (point B) with the team. They confirm staff attendance, set up/tear down requirements, processing sequence and, in the event where different lines are processing different product, then this work is allocated out. The start of shift meeting should be no longer than 10 or 15 minutes.

Depending on the production environment, the most effective tool I have seen for managing SIC is a large whiteboard secured firmly to the wall.

It has time interval columns pre-drawn on it with permanent ink. The supervisor then updates it with the day's production as discussed at the start of shift.

The white board will have three rows for each production line: the first for the plan, the second for the actual and the third for the variance.

Then on the appropriate SIC, the supervisor will review the "shop floor" and update the white board. This allows everyone to see how they are progressing. There are two scenarios:

1. **Staff is working too fast.** This may be good, but it may also mean that they are sacrificing quality for speed. Consider an operator on a line preparing chicken skewers. If they work too fast, they will not clean all the meat off the bone and the waste will be high.

2. **Staff is working too slowly.** On the other side, there is the operator working too slowly. This may be because of operational issues. The operator's station may be being fed raw product too slowly, it may be a skills issue or it may be attitudinal or a host of other problems.

In both situations the supervisor is required to take corrective action to bring the production output back onto plan. This is point C in the graphic. Ignoring the problem will result in a substantial variance at the end of the day: point E versus point D.

The most important point in all of this is that if you want to substantially increase productivity, then adopting SIC in some form or other is mandatory. It is often critiqued as being Taylorism in disguise. In the wrong hands, this critique may be true, but with common sense, it should never become a tool for driving punitive behaviour.

SIC does not only apply to supervisors and team leaders. It is applicable for all operational managers in all departments. The difference between the COO and the floor supervisor is that the COO has a longer interval between control points.

The Hierarchy of Dependent Objectives (HODO)

The all-important question is how the COO should be advised of the daily production. The answer is the Hierarchy of Dependent Objectives (HODO). The HODO was a term given to me by my late father to describe operational communications between levels of management.

Consider a business that has an aggregate forecasted demand of 240,000 units for the next 12 months. In the simplest of terms, the business will need to produce 20,000 units per month to meet demand.

To increase the complexity slightly, consider that the business has two production plants. This means that each plant should produce 10,000 units per month. Now consider that the business sells four different product types. Each plant is responsible for two lines. This means that each plant should produce 5000 units of each line per month. The plants must produce 1,250 units per week or 250 units per day or 34 units per hour (7.5 hour shift). So, if the business produces 34 units per hour across four products, across two plants, then it will meet the operational requirements of the business.

Let's overlay this with a typical operations organisation structure: the Chief Operating Officer (COO), Production Managers, Supervisors, Team Leaders and the workforce. The workforce is not treated as management. The following picture is the traditional hierarchy.

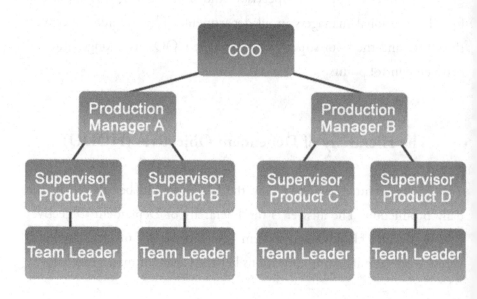

The picture below is the flow of information. Information is disaggregated **down** the hierarchy.

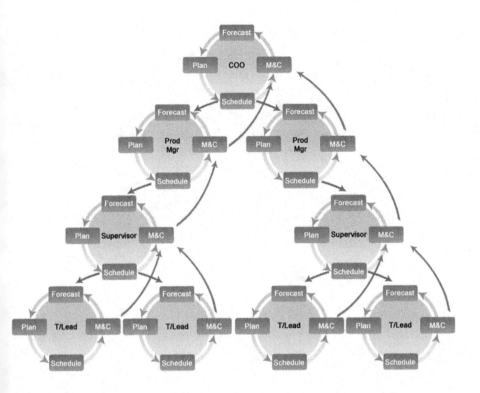

Note that *Schedule* goes to *Forecast*. This is vital as you cannot have lower level management working on an operational time line longer than that of the next level of senior management.

Information is aggregated **up** the hierarchy. These two information flows represent the hierarchy of dependent objectives (HODO).

Operationally it may very simplistically look like this:

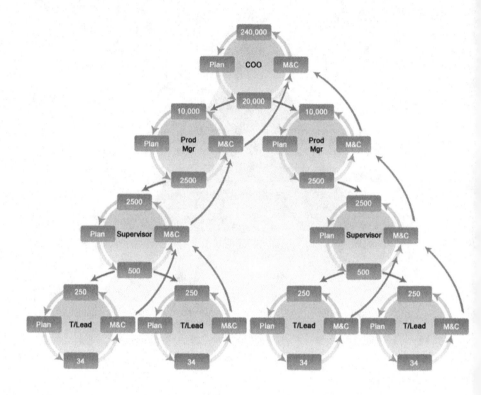

There are a number of key points here.

1. The management process is common for all levels of management.
2. Short Interval control is applicable to all levels of management.
3. If you do not have a formal schedule, then your measures may be a waste of time.
4. Without a formal review of Plan/Actual/Variance it is almost impossible to say if you have had a good day.

Customer Value Management

I was talking to a technology provider the other day who said they were having a tough time managing the expectations of their clients.

Throughout the conversation, they were questioning "the extra mile" they should go to address implementation and other project issues. My view was simple. Customer service is not defined by getting it right the first time; rather it is defined as how well you recover when you fail to get it right the first time. The company that goes the extra mile to recover a bad situation will always be thought of in a more positive light than the one that does not. It does not mean the relationship will always be saved, but generally it should result in neutral to positive press from the customer.

This conversation and the concept of customer service got me thinking about another topic that is close to my heart: the gulf between what businesses want and what customers value.

Businesses continually strive to do "more with less," to drive up profits or to meet a tightening budget. Customers on the other hand only ask to be valued: "Know who I am"; "Treat me with respect"; "Be professional in your dealings with me."

These two outcomes are generally exclusive. You can't do both. The manager's job is to find the balance. Part of this balance is recognising that you can't make everyone happy and there are customer profiles that just fall outside of the target market.

To delve into this more fully requires us to revisit first principles. Consider the following model. It represents the typical business view.

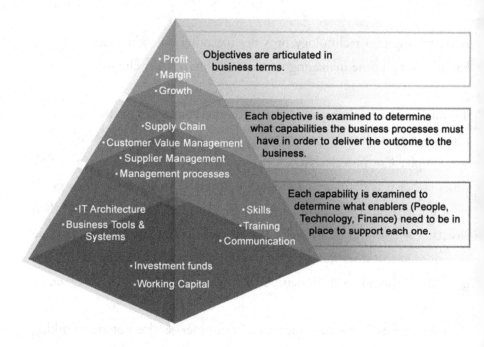

Source: Generic

Every business has its objectives: typically cost, quality and service. Business processes are designed to create the organisational capability required to meet these objectives. Investment is made in IT, People and Plant to enable the process capabilities. In less convoluted terms—*the enablers create the process capabilities required for the business to meet its objectives.*

On the other side of the ledger is the customer's view. Customers don't have objectives. They have values. "Know who I am," "Treat me with respect," and more.

So, the customer's model looks like this.

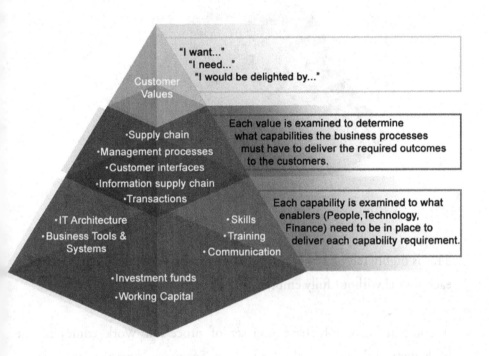

Source: IBM

There is obviously a high degree of overlap between the two models. In fact the only difference is at the "endgame," between the two interest groups. The objective is now to manage the inherent conflict between these two competing outcomes.

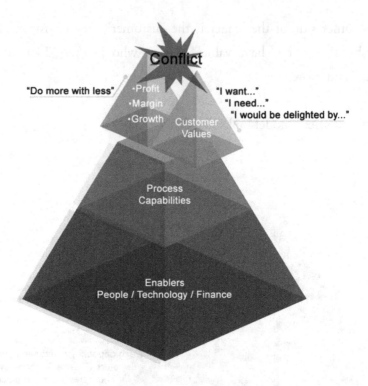

This is highly relevant as many businesses spend considerable time refining each model without fully embracing the common areas between them.

A company can only have one set of processes. Work comes in the back door and goes out the front door. So, when a manager is defining efficient processes for cost reduction they should simultaneously be defining the process for improved customer value management. This is less important for back office processes, but not unimportant.

Consider the credit check process. The customer does not care about the credit check. They just want to purchase their goods or service. The business wants to complete a credit check to avoid bad debts. The question is which process improvement action will create a better gross margin. Will it be reducing the process costs through headcount reduction, or increasing the process costs to reduce cycle time to minimise the time customers have to dwell on the fact you don't trust them and to change their mind about the purchase?

I realise the answer is to chase both outcomes. But a process is designed for the average and this exacerbates conflict.

How do you address specific transactions as they become "less average" and more complicated?

The initial answer is policy.

Policy allows you to treat customers as individuals, each on their own merits. But policy creates risk, training needs and recruitment needs.

Allied to this is the model by Zeithaml. His model describes five gaps between a business and the customer. These gaps are all relevant in minimizing the conflict noted above.

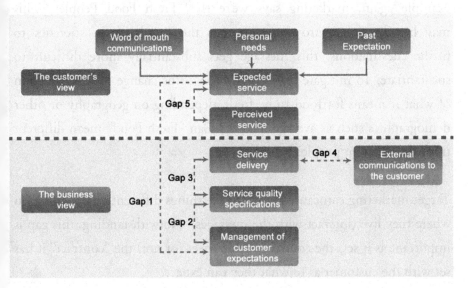

Source: Zeithaml

Gaps 1 and 4 are closely related, and they are the gulf between the messages a company creates and puts into the marketplace, and how those messages are interpreted by the customer. This includes the content and medium.

How a message is interpreted dictates the expectation by the customer of the type of service they can expect when dealing with that company. This gap is key, because everything follows from it. This is when we tell the customer what we will do and what to expect. It includes everything from direct conversations (over the counter/telephone, etc.) to corporate advertising. Consider: Optus says "Yes." That is a great marketing position aimed at the average. The individual that gets told "No" is going to have a different view of that message. Woolworths say they are the Fresh Food People. Not a good look when the weekend produce is not that fresh.

Gap 2 is between what the company is telling the customer they will do and what they are actually designing their processes to achieve. This is an internal gap between marketing and operations. Using my Woolworths example again, marketing says we're the "Fresh Food People." This may be true for metro stores, but as the supply chain stretches to further destinations, this message gets substantially more difficult to substantiate. To mitigate this, does Woolworths change the specification of what it means for food to be fresh, depending on geography or other demographics such as average income? Can "Fresh Food" mean different things to different people? I think it can.

Target marketing can cause people to see things differently depending on where they live (interact with the messages). Notwithstanding, this gap is important as it sets the company up to meet (or not) the "contract" it has set with the customer as to what they can expect.

Gap 3 is between the service quality specification and the actual delivery, as perceived by the business, not the customer.

For the record, I don't know if Woolworths changes their message for the country regions. The sign on the trucks stays the same. For this example I will assume that it does largely stay the same and that the quality of the produce sold in the country regions is not as good as that in the city.

From a business point of view, this is fine as you may get a higher margin in the city. From a customer value management point of view, this is fraught with danger. The country shopper who sees the message that says, "Fresh Food People" but due to supply chain issues, can't buy fresh food daily, may be forgiven for feeling undervalued and believing that Woolworths treats them as less important than the city folk. This was just an example. I used it as everyone understands what fresh food means. Again, I don't know how Woolworths manages country destinations. But it does highlight the need to minimise the gap between the marketing messages and the capability/capacity of the business operations.

Gap 5 is between the expected service quality and the actual delivery, as perceived by the customer. By managing gaps 1 and 4, the business has set an expectation of service quality in the customer's mind. Gap 5 is the determination by the customer as to whether they received the expected quality.

I believe the model could be extended to a sixth gap: namely the gap between how the customer expects the company to resolve a shortfall in service quality, and how it actually does.

In a previous lifetime I worked at a dairy as a brand manager. We would occasionally get complaints about the milk. Immediately on receiving the complaint, I would post the customer a card thanking them for taking the time to write in, and I would enclose two vouchers for free milk at their local.

An analysis of the complaints showed that more than half were due to problems beyond our control. In one instance we were not even the right dairy. But a follow-up with the customers showed a 100% satisfaction rating with our response.

The card, the vouchers, and the follow-up were much more expensive than a bottle of milk. But we kept the customer and they told their friends that we were a good company to do business with. This sixth gap is really overlooked. Millions of dollars are spent on winning and delighting customers, only to shortchange them when things go awry.

My opinion is that customers expect you to do what you said you would, and to fix it when it goes wrong.

KPIs, SLAs and Other Measurements

The concept of measuring business performance is not new. Successful companies have being doing it for hundreds of years.

As a junior consultant I was first introduced to measurement through the Philip Crosby school of total quality management. The lesson was simple: quality is defined as conformance to requirements. Define what you require and anything else is scrap, rework or waste.

Working with the (Alexander) Proudfoot management consultancy, I was taught "If you can't measure it, you can't manage it" and "If you control the parts you control the whole."

These authors were promoting their thinking on these topics around 1960. Over the last 50 years the measurement industry has exploded and the need to have measures in a business is now largely considered mandatory. But the activity of the last 50 years has also clouded the issue. There are so many schools of thought and so many voices in the market that the foundation intent for having measurement has become blurred, confused and generally mired in consultant speak.

My view on measurement recognises four frames:

1. External
2. Horizontal
3. Vertical
4. Community

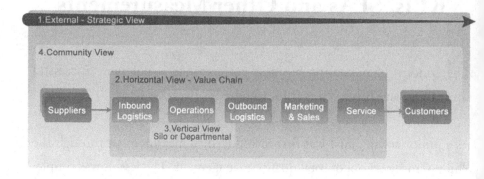

- The external view is the strategic view.
- The horizontal view is the internal value chain.
- The vertical view is the departments and silos within a business.
- The community view is the relationship with suppliers and customers—the extended value chain.

Each frame requires a different type of thinking and approach to measurement as influenced by the following variables:

1. Nature of decision-making:
a) Strategic
b) Operational

An understanding of the nature and impact of decisions that will be made as a consequence of the performance measures will assist in defining what measures should be included in the scorecard. It is important to consider how the behaviour will change as a result of "knowing the answer." If you measure things that you have no means of responding to, then it is not worth measuring them at all.

2. Organisational position:
a) Scope/influence of authority within the business
b) Time horizon—short, medium, long-term

The more senior a manager, the more influential their decision-making authority is and the medium and long-term become increasingly important. Seniority within the business will also dictate whether lead or lag indicators should be more or less important to a manager.

3. Measurement type:
a) Key performance indicators (KPI)
b) Service level agreements (SLA)
c) Working level agreements (WLA)

I consider three measurement types to be relevant to the business community. (The IT community may include a few extra types.)

4. Accountability:
a) Team
b) Individual

This variable addresses who is accountable for the indicator. As seniority increases, accountability moves from the individual to the team. In my view, executive managers should be evaluated as a team and not as individuals.

To consolidate these variables:

View	Decision making	Organisational influence	Time indicator	Type	Accountability
External	Strategic	Authority	Lead	KPI	Team
Horizontal	Operational	Time	Lag	SLA	Individual
Vertical				WLA	
Community					

The Horizontal View

This view is characterised by the principle that it is more important to manage the future than it is to manage the past. Or, in more colloquial terms, to ensure the light in the tunnel is not a train.

The dominant characteristics are highlighted:

View	Decision making	Organisational influence	Time indicator	Type	Accountability
External	Strategic	Authority	Lead	KPI	Team
Horizontal	Operational	Time	Lag	SLA	Individual
Vertical				WLA	
Community					

To have a horizontal view in a business automatically implies seniority (mid-level management and above) and a high-performing value chain requires the management group to work together as a team and for the team to take collective responsibility for the performance of the value chain.

The need for a high-performing team is so important that the relationships should be managed by Working Level Agreements (WLAs). WLAs recognise that the individual manager within the team has limited authority and the success of the team therefore relies on each manager to be fully contributing their share to the success of the value chain. The WLA is the contract/agreement between the parts of the internal value chain. (I recognise that this relationship can be managed by SLAs. It's only a question of terminology and scope.)

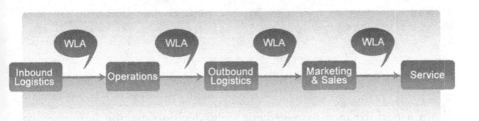

At this level, lead indicators are more important. For example, the number of purchase orders issued is a lead indicator to operational health. If you are not buying anything, then you are going to run out of production material and the business will stop. Accounts receivable and debtor days are lead indicators to financial health. If you are not creating debt (selling) and/or not collecting the debt, then you are going out of business. Inventory holdings are lead indicators to sales. Increasing inventory potentially means sales are falling off and the business is running out of working capital.

Typically lead indicators are characterised by volume as defined by their unit of measure, being generally either units or currency i.e., volume of purchase orders issued. Total value of purchase orders issued is another example, as are total inventory holdings and total value of inventory.

The team should have a set of KPIs for the value chain for which they are collectively responsible. These KPIs measure the value created through the value chain.

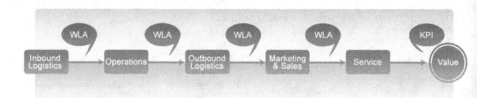

From a performance management view, decision-making is operational. Strategic decisions such as insource/outsource are made to impact specific operational performance measures.

The Vertical View

The vertical view has a restrictive scope and applies to specific departments, divisions or sub sections thereof.

The dominant characteristics are highlighted in the table below:

View	Decision making	Organisational influence	Time indicator	Type	Accountability
External	Strategic	Authority	Lead	KPI	Team
Horizontal	Operational	Time	Lag	SLA	Individual
Vertical				WLA	
Community					

To have a vertical view in the business is to work in a silo. The focus is on the manager's specific area of accountability. An important differentiator between the vertical and horizontal view is that the vertical view is equally applicable to all levels of management, from team supervisors to executives and the horizontal view is across functions at a senior level in the organisation.

It is not uncommon for executives to use the same indicator as a lag indicator for their portfolio and a lead indicator for the value chain. But at the lower levels of management and supervision this duality does not exist. Here the question is "How can we do more with less?" The focus is on process efficiency and examining why process targets were not met. Supervisors will ask, "What went wrong and how can we do better next time?"

Accountability is at the individual level. "This is your department—you are responsible for what happens in it."

A team environment does exist, except that it is a vertical team e.g., the Finance team or the operations team. The team relies on each other to manage their sub departments and the KPIs for each sub department are a disaggregation of the overall departments' performance indicators. This relationship is termed the Hierarchy of Dependent Objectives (HODO) and is described earlier in the book.

The volume flows measured as lead indicators for the value chain become the volume drivers for setting resource levels and measuring asset productivity with lag indicators.

The Community View

The community view recognises the importance of third-party customers and suppliers and their relationship to the business.

The dominant characteristics are highlighted in the table below:

View	Decision making	Organisational influence	Time indicator	Type	Accountability
External	Strategic	Authority	Lead	KPI	Team
Horizontal	Operational	Time	Lag	SLA	Individual
Vertical				WLA	
Community					

These relationships are different from the horizontal view, in that neither the supplier nor customer has authority over the other. The supplier is contracted (formally or informally) to provide services to the customer. (Services include the delivery of product.) The contract is managed by monitoring adherence to service levels (SLAs) imposed on the supplier by the customer. Typically these will include performance measures on Time, Cost and Quality.

The more the supplier and customer can work as a team, the better the relationship will be. In this case the relationship can be managed with a combined scorecard. The customer will use lag indicators to measure the supplier's performance and the supplier will use lead indicators to evaluate the viability/health of the relationship.

In the event that the two parties do not have a team-based relationship, then the customer is likely to manage with lag indicators and to show little regard for the supplier's lead indicators.

It is also common that SLAs are used within a business and this does not conflict with the community view. The internal, interdepartmental relationships at the process level often require SLAs to manage them. WLAs manage the value chain; SLAs manage the inter process relationships.

Typically process level SLAs are best suited for managing the relationship between the front and back offices—or the customer facing, revenue generating processes and the non-customer facing, revenue support processes. These are different from the foundation processes that are removed from the customer altogether.

The customer facing process triggers the customer facing support process to start. This process must complete in an agreed time and produce an output of agreed quality at an agreed cost. Adherence to this Cost/Quality/Time combination allows the customer facing process (role) to make promises to the external customer that can be relied on.

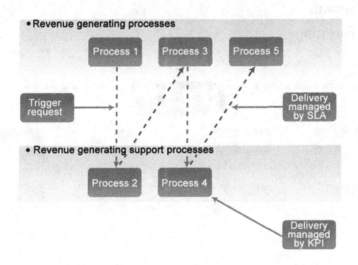

Here KPIs are used within the process and SLAs are managing the relationship between the processes and every formal SLA requires an equally formal trigger.

The Strategic View

The strategic view encompasses the entire business or major operating divisions within the company, depending on the size of the company. The dominant characteristics are highlighted.

View	Decision making	Organisational influence	Time indicator	Type	Accountability
External	Strategic	Authority	Lead	KPI	Team
Horizontal	Operational	Time	Lag	SLA	Individual
Vertical				WLA	
Community					

For a company, the objective is to increase shareholder and stakeholder value. There are four primary drivers for this:

- Profitability
- Productivity
- Growth
- Financing

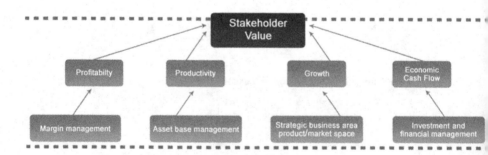

I discuss this model in depth separately in the book.

Governance

Understanding Organisational Governance

As with all of the business models I have written about, organisational governance has been well documented by other authors. And for every author there is a definition.

I define governance as the **proactive management of variance**, applied equally to **compliance** and **performance**. I address risk separately, later in the article.

The two halves of governance are equally important yet it seems that whenever I read articles or hear conversations on the subject, they are always referring to compliance.

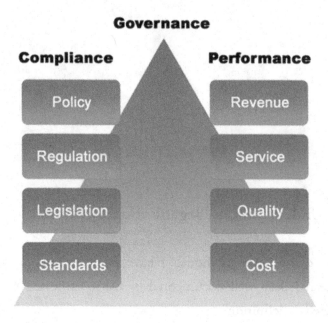

Compliance is the activity where the company ensures adherence to its own *internal* policies and standards, and to the policies, standards, regulation and legislation imposed on it by *external* industry bodies, and local, national and international law.

Performance refers to ensuring operational processes adhere to the internal standards for revenue, cost, quality and service, or put more simply, ensuring that operations are working to budget.

There are two important truths here:

1. You can have process without compliance, but you cannot have compliance without process, and
2. You can have process without management, but you cannot have management without process.

It is therefore the **business process** that binds compliance and performance together.

The role of management is to ensure business processes adhere to budget and to address variances as they arise. This is true for all managers irrespective of their position or role in the organisation.

The reverse is equally true: as compliance functions are expected to manage to budget (i.e. performance), operations functions can be expected to manage to the restrictions imposed by compliance frameworks.

This therefore raises the question: why does the term "governance" get used so widely and have so much importance placed on it? If managers accept that their role embraces both performance and compliance, then governance and management should be considered one and the same thing, and the apparent separation disappears.

Many of my clients have employed managers for compliance specific roles, such as an OH&S manager or a sustainability manager. There is nothing wrong with these appointments; indeed they are most necessary. These managers are employed as subject matter experts to own a portfolio (such as OH&S) and to be responsible for how that portfolio manifests itself in the business. This includes being responsible for knowledge transfer, awareness, training etc. and all the other dimensions that a subject matter expert can bring to the business.

They are also accountable for the appropriateness of the framework they use and for managing how well the business adheres to the compliance processes associated with their portfolio. In essence, they are responsible for managing how well the business complies with its own compliance regime.

What they are **not** responsible for is the active management of compliance in the business. Here the operational process managers are responsible. The operational manager is responsible for not only what gets produced by the process, but also how the output is produced. In this case, the "how" is defined by the restrictions imposed on the production process by any and all of the applicable compliance frameworks. Process managers don't get to choose which framework they will and won't adhere to.

The Compliance Framework

To further explore the idea of compliance frameworks, a framework is a model and a filter and importantly a model is only an abstract. It is an alternative way to see the business. It is not the business itself. Every framework is different and each allows a manager to view specific aspects of the business and to filter out all those aspects of the business that they are not interested in.

Every compliance manager has their preferred framework. Popular frameworks include the eTom for Telecommunications, ITIL for IT, APQC for business analysts and Sarbanes Oxley for Finance. These frameworks all manage risk in some way. Then there are the risk frameworks themselves which get treated as something different again.

While each framework is different, the business is consistent. It doesn't change, no matter which framework you use. Consider the following illustration of a generic enterprise.

In this "naked" view, it does not matter who is looking at the business. Everybody sees the same thing. If you apply views/filters you get the following. The filters are examples only.

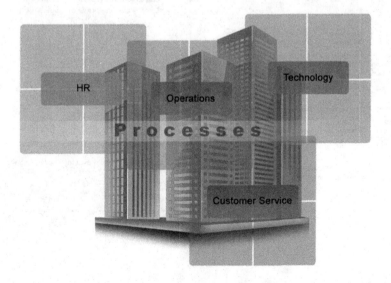

It is the same business, but now seen through the selected view of the manager's choice. These views do not corrupt the message. Rather they focus it to remove "noise" and other irrelevant data. But it is clear that if a manager is looking at the business through an HR view, then they are not looking at it through an IT view. This tends to create silos, in that managers start to only see the business through one view and forget that it is only a view and not the business. Working in teams helps mitigate this issue.

Frameworks guide the manager in the matter of what should be considered when transacting the business process and which parts of the processes need to be controlled to ensure that the business is adhering to its internal policies and applicable external regulations, legislations etc.

For example, the COSO framework requires a business to define itself in four categories: Finance, Sales and Operations, Corporate and Legal Affairs, and HR.

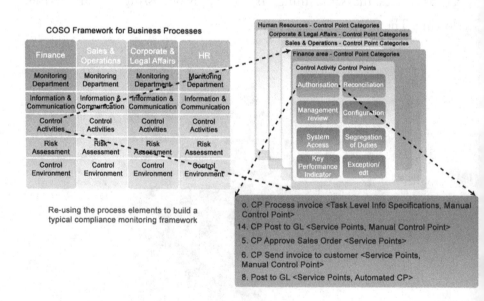

For each of these categories there are sub categories and so on and so forth. The drill down process stops when it gets to the business process. At this point, specific process steps in the transactional process are identified as control points to ensure that the process will deliver an outcome consistent with the requirements of the framework.

The compliance manager owns the framework, but the business process manager is accountable for ensuring adherence to the control points. Their daily/weekly/monthly process KPIs should include validation that the control points are being managed correctly.

This is fairly straightforward when a manager is dealing with one compliance framework. It gets more complicated when the same process step is the control point for multiple frameworks.

To manage this complexity the risk manager should own and manage a repository of control points. The repository will detail the many-to-many relationships between Risk, Framework, Process, Process Control Points, Process Managers and Process Owners.

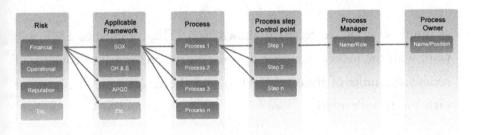

This spectrum tells the *process owner* what control points they should be managing in each of the processes in their portfolio; and it tells the *risk manager* who they should be working through to mitigate each of the risks. It highlights which process steps are key control points in that they are governed by more than one compliance framework. The relevant compliance manger ensures that the responsible managers have the skills and tools to manage the control points.

The organisation model could look like this:

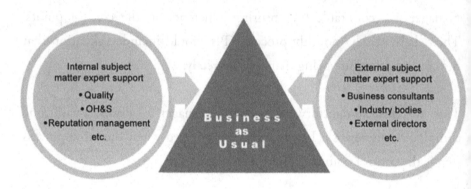

Once the repository model is established and the relationships known, then the process manager should use a scorecard to manage the control points in exactly the same manner as they manage process performance using KPIs, short interval control and analysis of variance.

A simple example scorecard is shown next. The compliance SME will work with the process manager to agree on the appropriate frequency of review, the units of measure (UOM) and the target score (budget) for each compliance metric.

					Actuals					Cumulative		
	Manager								Year	2012		
									Month			
KPA		KPI	UOM	Freq	Planned	Week1	Week2	Week3	Week4	Week5	Planned	Actual	Variance
Department/Division/Org Unit	Performance	KPA 1	Metric 1	Hr	W									
			Metric 2	Hr	W									
			Metric 3	Hr	W									
		KPA 2	Metric 4	#	W									
			Metric 5	$	W									
			Metric 6	#	W									
			Metric 7	$	W									
			Metric 8	#	W									
			Metric 9	%	W									
			Metric 10	#	W									
		KPA 3	Metric 11	#	W									
			Metric 12	$										
			Metric 13	#	W									
			Metric 14	$										
			Metric 15	#	W									
			Metric 16	$	W									
	Compliance	Control type	Metric 17	#	W									
		Control type	Metric 18	Hrs	W									
			Metric 19	#	W									

In my opinion, it is not an overly long bow to treat a scorecard as just another framework.

There are many opinions on what's an appropriate organisation structure to manage the marriage between performance and compliance. Operational performance generally reports through to the COO. Compliance is all about risk and the risk manager should be accountable for the means by which risk is understood by the business. This includes ensuring the use of appropriate frameworks. By extension compliance managers should report to the risk manager and the risk manager should apply a very broad definition to the word "risk."

This raises the question—who should the risk manager report to? The answer is largely determined by the nature and culture of the business and the strength of the need to separate operations from risk. In certain circumstances it will be acceptable for the risk manager to report to the COO; in other cases this would be akin to asking the fox to install the chicken wire. Other reporting lines can be through the CFO or directly to the CEO.

For such a structure to work requires effective matrix management. It also requires operational managers to take the time to fully understand the processes they are responsible for and to embrace their wider responsibility in terms of risk and compliance management.

In closing it is worth reinforcing the point that effective governance/management requires the adherence to multiple frameworks. One framework cannot do it all. Equally to allow, or cause, a manager to focus predominately or solely on performance is to undermine the wider role of management in the business.

To Grow Shareholder Wealth

By way of acknowledgement, the model I use in this chapter was given to me by my MBA lecturer, the late Michael Halliday. I found it at the back of a reading he asked us to look at:

> Shareholder value creation can be defined as the process of building lasting economic value for a corporation's shareholders and key stakeholders such as the employees, customers, suppliers, financiers and society.

> The problem is that the objectives of the shareholders and stakeholders are often different and most likely in conflict with each other. These differences stem from the fact that while managers face the daily challenge of maximising sales, profit and market share, third party institutions generally own the majority of shares.

> This creates a separation of ownership and control. Theory has it that managers are the agents of the owners and in a perfect world the share price would reflect the present value of all future activities the company and good management practice would drive up the share price.

In reality, institutions are judged on the short term performance of their portfolios and they therefore pressure management to deliver high increases in the short term.

This in turn causes business managers to adopt inappropriate management practices at the expense of the mid to long term.

The above quote refers to public companies. But I believe it is equally true for private companies. The difference is that in private companies, the owner is the manager. And, as such, time pressures (quarterly reporting) are reduced and there is less scrutiny on his/her behaviour and decision-making. But in practice, the endgame for both types of company is the same—namely value creation.

There are four primary drivers of organisational value: Profitability, Productivity, Cash Flow and Strategic Growth.

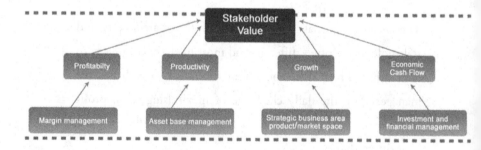

Based on a model by Michael Halliday

These four drivers are of equal importance and it is difficult to pick a start point.

You need cash, otherwise you can't start, but you also need a market and a business, otherwise you can't apply your cash. You may have identified your market, but if you don't have a sales proposition, then you won't sell and you won't place demand on your assets (productivity).

I will start with **Growth**.

Growth represents the markets that you trade in or plan to enter. Ansoff articulated it well with his grid, as follows:

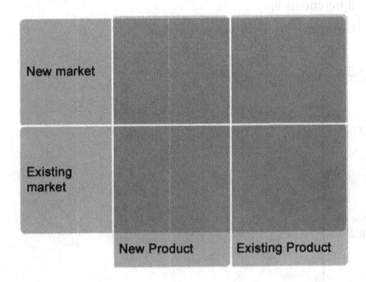

Source: Ansoff

The options are to take a new or existing product into a new market, or to further develop the existing market through better positioning of an existing product—or the introduction of a new product.

The strategic choice between these options is: diversification or differentiation.

This paper focuses on differentiation only—improving returns from an existing market.

Differentiation is the easier of the two strategies, as the market already knows who you are and is preconditioned to trust your products.

With differentiation the manager has two choices at their disposal.

1. Compete through better product positioning. Degree of differentiation.
2. Compete through cost leadership.

Consider the following graph:

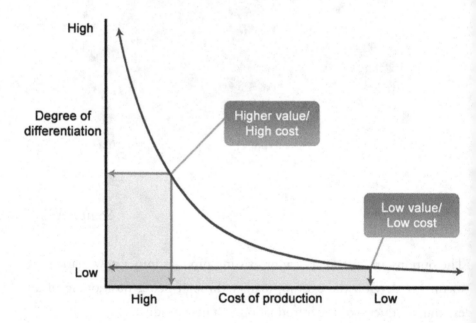

Source: Unknown

On the Y axis is the degree of differentiation. How are the products or services positioned and perceived in the market? Is the product positioned as "tailor-made" or is it seen as a "commodity" or smewhere in between?

The scale[1] is as follows:

1. Commodity
2. Quality
3. Exclusive
4. Tailor-made

The more a product is positioned and perceived as exclusive or tailor-made, the more the market will pay for it.

A product positioned as tailor-made is developed for a specific individual according to their specific needs. This by its nature is highly differentiated and very expensive.

On the X axis is cost leadership. How cheaply can you sell your product or service? This automatically positions the product as a commodity. The strategy is high sales volume.

Traditionally you can't have both and these two axes work inversely to each other. The more you differentiate, the more it costs.

To differentiate your product in an existing market requires that you know how it is positioned relative to the rest of the market. Consider the following example market plot.

---

[1]   I first saw this scale while working with IBM.

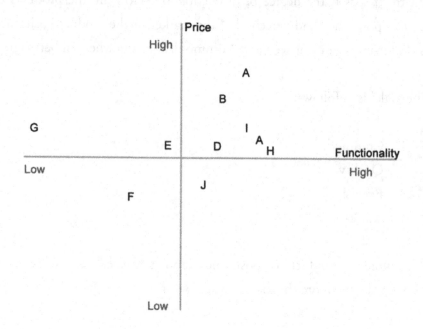

Source: Generic model

The X axis is functionality and the Y axis is price. Both axes are rated high/low. The plots represent the product positioning in the market. There are some great toolsets in the market to assist with this type of analysis.

The plot identifies open areas, where there are few or no products. These areas represent the opportunity to either reposition your existing product or launch a new product to fill the void.

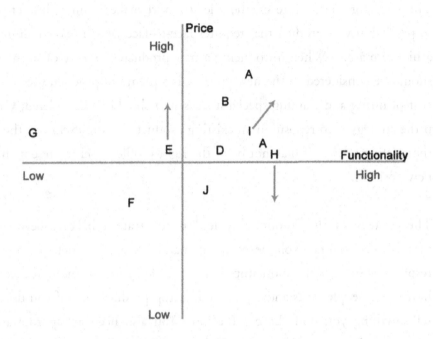

The risk is that existing products (including your own) have an existing position in the market and customers understand this. If the distance from the current position to the new position is too great, the customer will become confused and it is likely you will lose sales. For "greater distances" it is better to launch a new product that is clearly different from the existing products.

This type of repositioning happens in the "profitability" leg. The growth leg determines which markets you will sell in; the profitability leg determines how you will sell to that market. The primary levers for product (re)positioning are:

1. Pricing
2. Sales approach
3. Sales support

The need for, and nature of, the sales support makes a huge difference to profitability. A product that requires face-to-face sales support requires a higher margin. When introducing a new product, this type of support should be considered. If the new product is a premium product, then the cost of hiring and training specialist sales staff should be considered. Or, if the strategy is to reposition an existing product as more exclusive, then the existing sales staff may not be of the right profile to sell/represent the new position.

The strategy of the "profitability leg" is to create a balance between margin and volume. Volume equals demand for the product. In many respects, volume is the most important variable in the business. You can have great people, outstanding marketing, top products, but if you don't sell anything you don't have a business. You also need an appropriate return for the product or service. If the margin is high, then the volume can be low. This is perfectly acceptable in a business designed for low volumes. But in many cases a high margin is not enough. Volume must be high as well. Consider a $1 product that produces an 80% margin. Good margin, but no money.

Volume is the primary driver for the "productivity leg." To compete on cost requires a focus on Asset Productivity. A key measure is Return on Capital Employed.

Consider the following four assets:

1. Human Resources
2. Machinery/Plant/Facilities
3. Money/Finance/Treasury
4. Inventory

These four assets are the tangible side of the business. Improving the yield (productivity) from these assets will grow the value of the business.

Productivity is measured as an input: output ratio. Therefore to improve productivity the options are:

1. Same input: improved output
2. Increase input: increase output beyond the increased input
3. Decrease input: maintain output (or small decrease in output).

The inputs are the assets. The output is the product or service that the customer buys.

Earlier in the chapter I noted the need to create demand for the business and that the "legs" of growth and profitability create demand. In this case, demand means demand for the output of the business. The manager's job is to maintain and grow this demand and to work the assets to maintain a target productivity ratio.

Unfortunately, most managers only have control over the assets and not the marketplace. By marketplace I mean the sales and marketing initiatives of the company. This means that most managers have little control over the creation of demand for the assets in their managerial portfolio, and the only lever they can pull (especially when times are tough) is option 3—the cost reduction lever or decreased asset input. This often results in layoffs as the human asset is the easiest one to move and is the asset that delivers immediate cost reductions.

But if the business wants to lower the cost of production whilst maintaining its point of differentiation then I recommend a model I picked up from IBM called the dynamic stability model.

The way it works is to separate marketing from production.

As discussed previously strategic product marketing is broken down into four segments:

1. Commodity
2. Quality
3. Exclusive
4. Tailor-made

From a production point of view there is:

1. Mass production
2. Continuous improvement
3. Invention
4. Mass customisation

Prevailing wisdom says that these concepts are closely aligned. "Tailor-made" requires "Invention" and "Commodity" requires "Mass production."

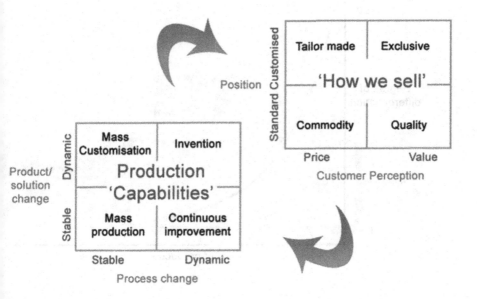

Source: IBM

The strategy is to break the connection between the two concepts. In the extreme this means that you set up a mass production environment for a tailor-made product.

Mass production reduces the cost of producing the product. Tailor-made maximises the value of the item. The difference is a maximisation of the gross margin of the product. If you can keep a mass production environment working, the assets have little to no downtime and the productivity ratio will be high.

Stakeholder value is created when a business is able to lower the cost of production without compromising the point of differentiation. This is the *ideal position* and it represents the point at which the company can charge a premium price and take an inflated gross margin.

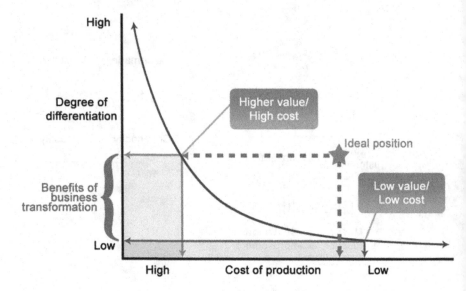

It is one thing to know what to do. It is another thing to pay for it. This introduces the last leg of the model—finances. Finance is relatively straightforward. You have two options:

1. Debt
2. Equity

It is vital to understand the assumptions behind the venture before making the financing decision. It is common for entrepreneurs, managers and business analysts to build an investment spreadsheet and consider that it reflects what will happen in real life.

On paper it all seems reasonable, but will it happen in practise? The devil is in the detail. To validate the model I suggest the following sequence:

1. Write down the assumptions you have made about the business.
2. Build a model based on these assumptions.

3. Hold an open workshop with trusted advisers to rigorously challenge the assumptions.
4. Refine the model and prepare a sensitivity analysis on the key variables.
5. Produce a final answer.

It is important to not only validate the written assumptions, but equally or more important to validate assumptions that are not there. What has the author missed? What's not written down?

If you have an existing business then the model should focus on the planned extension to the business. In other words, could the extension stand on its own merits? If it cannot, you could be growing revenue but diluting gross margin. If it can, what synergies will you pick up by merging the new with the existing business?

The answer is really the least of your worries. Do not anticipate it; do not rush it. A rushed model will provide the answers you want rather than the answer you need.

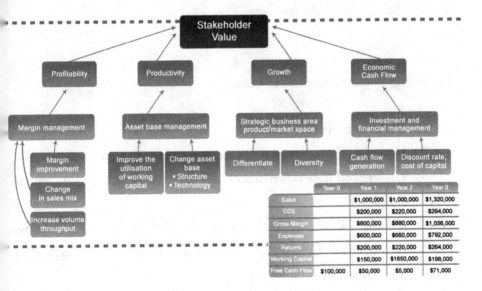

Once you have the answer you are now in a position to determine your source of funds. I acknowledge the model will need to include funding options in order to take into account interest expense. But you should model with a "switch" to turn this option on or off.

If the model indicates stable growth and there is confidence in the assumptions, then debt is probably the way to go. If it appears that the venture will require a "long runway" to get off the ground then equity may make more sense, depending on whether or not you can fund the interest payments on debt. My experience is that things always take longer to materialise than expected and if you go the debt option, allow yourself a good cushion of time.

It must be said that equity is the most expensive form of money. Not in terms of dividends etc., but when it comes to selling the asset. What at the start seems like a reasonable equity percentage could become a very big payout figure at the end. A good equity partner should assist the business and help it grow. Often investors have great management skills and can bring a lot to the business.

In closing, to grow shareholder value:

1. Understand your markets.
2. Understand how you will create demand from those markets.
3. Understand how this demand will improve the Return on Capital Employed.
4. Choose a financing methodology that will support your business through the difficult first years but will not be too expensive when it comes time to exit.

Managing Change

Background

My views on change management were forged by the 14 months I spent on the Mercedes Benz South Africa (MBSA) project. The project ran for a few years commencing in 1995.

The date is relevant, as the country had just started taking its first steps as a full democracy. The memory of the apartheid years was fresh in the minds of all, and those of the local labour force, most of whom had borne the brunt of some of the worst aspects of the apartheid regime.

The project was a large transformation project affecting most areas of the business. Success could only be achieved if the workforce supported the transformation and, based on the country's recent history, this level of trust would be very difficult to achieve.

An important point to note: this article in no way implies that MBSA supported or endorsed the apartheid regime. Rather, the difficulties I refer to were experienced by the workers on a daily basis just by living in the country.

The MBSA Project

A project team was assembled with experts flying in from all over the world. MBSA allocated approximately 70 full-time staff to the project.

We kicked off the project with a three-day off-site conference. The agenda was to make sure that everyone on the team understood the vision, the methodology and the toolsets we would be using. (There was also time for team-building, normally over a bottle of Meerlust Rubicon '77, a particularly fine wine.)

The project followed the normal course of any large transformation. Data collection, analysis, visioning etc. Interlaced throughout this activity was a change management program.

The program employed a number of communication techniques including everything from posters and brochures, to live theatre and town hall meetings.

The posters and brochures were professionally produced, multilingual and widely distributed. The theatre was delivered by professional actors. The themes were designed to mimic how MBSA treated their customers and the consequential customer reaction. It was very confronting. This theatre was played out in all locations all over the country. It told the story of why change was necessary.

The town hall meetings were carefully managed affairs often held at an outside venue. The conference rooms were transformed with MBSA branding—and when you stepped into the room, you knew you were somewhere special. The meetings were also held all over the country, so every location felt included. This meant that MBSA often had the entire transformation team and scores of staff and management driving or flying hundreds of kilometres. The cost would have been enormous. Typically an event would have 500 people in attendance.

At each session the Managing Director would make a presentation acknowledging issues and/or describing the future. The trade unions were invited to these sessions and were privy to all the presentations.

The intent of the communications package was to ensure that everyone in the organisation was aware of the need for change, what could be expected from the project and how they could communicate their concerns back to management.

For me, the crowning moment of the change management program was when the trade union members stood up—unannounced—at a town hall meeting, and started singing songs of support for the program. What was once an adversarial relationship was quickly becoming a relationship based on respect and a common desire to address the issues in the company. It was a highly emotional moment and instantly became my benchmark for what a well-orchestrated change management program could achieve.

In summary the characteristics of the MBSA change management program were:

1. A well-funded, well-staffed, cohesive project team.
2. A well-funded, dedicated change program.
3. A broad selection of communication techniques catering for all levels of literacy and learning preferences.

4. A substantial allocation of time to the change program.
5. Strong participation and leadership from the Managing Director down.
6. Management went to the people. (Staff was not called to a head office presentation.)
7. Honesty.
8. Willingness to actively listen and respond to feedback.

What we can learn

In the time since the Mercedes Benz South Africa project, I have not seen another like it. The major difference between MBSA and subsequent projects I have witnessed is the restriction on time and money. Project leaders almost always acknowledge the need for a dedicated change management program but frequently this desire does not translate into sufficient funds, time or active engagement from the leadership. Mostly a business will hire a change manager and consider the change management job done. But just because you have a change manager does not mean you have a change program.

Two dimensions to change management

There are two dimensions to change management.

The first dimension is the organisational level view. The second is recognition of each individual in the business.

The first engages the hearts and minds of all stakeholders. The focus is on establishing a common and pervasive understanding of the need for change, and then ensuring that each person is aware of their responsibilities in assisting change to happen.

The second is actually changing the behaviour of the individual. Even with a comprehensive change management program, it does not mean that an individual will actually decide to modify their behaviour.

Effective change management at the organisational level requires that the business give it a formal mandate. This means that its importance is recognised and that it has a formal structure.

An effective change management structure typically has four levels:

1. The steering committee
2. The working committee
3. The project teams
4. The program office

The **steering committee** sets the project strategy and ensures the projects are delivering change in line with the strategic intent of the company.

The **working committee** is the primary engine for driving change in the business. Its purpose is to establish and manage the project teams that will gather and synthesise data and then to discuss this data and make recommendations to the steering committee.

The **project teams** are task-focused groups, typically made up of staff members who have been seconded full-time to the project, part-time subject matter experts and business consultants who may provide methodology and other specialist skills.

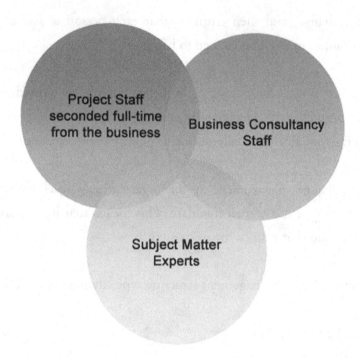

The **program office** ensures this change hierarchy is managed for success. It provides the tools and resources, and allocates the budget to ensure the desired outcomes can be achieved. It should restrict its role to librarian and scorekeeper. It is not on the field of play, but watching the play. This ensures that it does not inadvertently impede the business from taking ownership of change. It is important to note that the business *provides* the budget. The program office *allocates* the budget.

Putting it all together you get:

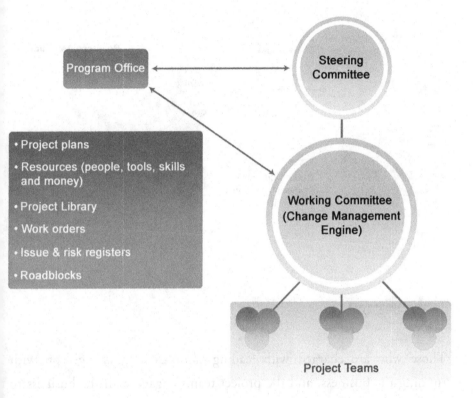

The project teams can either be orientated by function or service line, i.e., a finance team that examines everything in finance, or a process team that examines all processes in the business. In the former, the subject matter expert is the process person and in the latter the subject matter expert is the finance representative.

I consider it essential that one of the project teams is a communications team, with the sole focus of communicating the "project" to the business and ensuring that the business can communicate with the project.

Bringing "business as usual" into the picture you get:

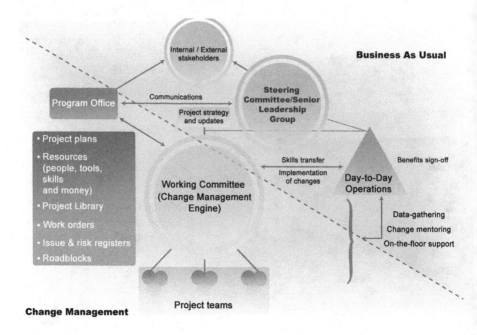

Those who are charged with leading *"business as usual"* get on with running the business, and the project teams engage with the business to better understand the issues and discuss improvements.

If the business is willing to fully formalise this approach then the above structure will include a corrective action team (CAT) as a second essential project team. The various project teams can come and go as required, but the CAT and the communications team become permanent fixtures.

Many project leaders I speak to consider their projects to be too small for such a formal communications management role. To mitigate this constraint, the communications process should still be formalised, but the staffing becomes part-time.

I learnt a long time ago the formula for rumour. It is rumour = ambiguity x interest.

With a project there is always interest. Good communications will dilute the ambiguity.

There are two aspects to preparing a structured communications package. These are the message itself and the management of the message. Each has sub attributes.

Message	Management
Content	Collect
Relevance	Store
Accuracy	Process
Timeliness	Distribute
Access	
Support	

For the message, consider:

- Who is going to read the content and why is it relevant to them?
- What is the level of accuracy required?
- Will broad brush statements suffice or is it important to include numbers to the second decimal point?
- When is the information needed and how will it be accessed?
- If there are questions, who do they turn to for support?

The answers to these questions will determine the physical attributes of the message.

For example, a senior executive is accustomed to working with electronic messages anywhere in the world. A factory worker may want to be addressed personally in a town hall meeting, where they can evaluate first-hand the "trustworthiness" of the messenger. Management of the message includes answering the questions: Where does the raw data come from? How do I reply to it? Where/how can I access it at a later stage?

To briefly summarise the concept behind the corrective action team, the business gets on with day-to-day operations. When non-conformance to requirements is identified through normal business activity, then it is up to the management structure to address the issue. In the event that they are not able to permanently resolve the underlying issue that caused the non-conformance, then they will raise a CAR (corrective action request) and lodge it with the CAT. The CAT will work with the other project teams to fully diagnose the underlying issue and will recommend actions to the working committee to permanently resolve the problem. The working committee reviews and endorses the recommendations and the business is asked to implement the change and to monitor its effectiveness. The project teams should assist with implementation.

As this corrective action process gets better and stronger, a culture of continuous improvement emerges and the change management structure evolves and transforms from being a vehicle set up to deliver a project to become a vehicle that delivers excellence in the business.

This brings us to the **second dimension of change management—** changing the individual.

When a person is asked to change their routine and habits they generally go through three stages of change (Source: Proudfoot).

Suitable terms for these stages are:

1. Mechanistic
2. Conceptual
3. Adoption

Source Proudfoot Plc

The **mechanistic** stage is the toughest. This is when an individual is most resistant to change. They are questioning the relevance of the change, and often say that while they fully support the change, it does not apply to their role. Often staff will attend meetings or training on the new approach and be positive in the session. Afterwards they return to their work area and tell their staff, "That's all rubbish, those folk in their fancy suits don't know what they are talking about and it will never work here. We will continue doing what we have always done."

To resolve this mind-set the change manager needs to work with the individual staff members and often the best approach is JFDI: "Just do it." The individual is forced to comply. They do not have to fully understand why the change is important; they only have to adopt the new way of doing things.

Over a period of time—which could be hours, days or weeks—the penny will drop, and the staff member will start to see the benefits of doing it the new way.

This is the second stage—**conceptual understanding**. At this point they will start to introduce positive improvements and customisations to make the changes more relevant and appropriate to their area.

As this happens they move to the third stage—**adoption.** They now have full ownership of the changes and consider them their own. Asking them to make further changes at this time becomes difficult as they will be back to stage 1.

To move a person through these three stages requires extensive "on-the-floor" support. The change agent needs to be working with the business on a daily basis to help implement the changes.

The expected level of resistance can be plotted in the following matrix:

	Can	Can't
Will	Encourage Role model Use as change leader	On-the-job training Mentor Celebrate achievement
Won't	Counsel Support On-the-job mentoring	Counsel Consider reallocation to other duties

Source: Generic

The key is to identify those staff that **Can** work in the new way of doing things and who **Will** work with you and use them as change leaders/role models. These staff members require the least amount of effort.

Staff that **Will** work with you but lack the skills to do so (**Can't**) are the next easiest group. Their minds are open and they are willing to learn. Give them training and mentoring to embed the new routines. It is important not to underestimate the amount of time these people need to embed the change. Without on-going mentoring, the changes may become too difficult and the person may slip into the **Won't/Can't** category.

The third category is **Can/Won't**. This person has the skills to work in the new way but is resistant to doing so. They are firmly entrenched in stage 1. This person is most dangerous to the change program. Other staff will watch how this person is dealt with and may take their lead from him/her. This person requires extensive "on-the-floor" support and the JFDI approach should be strictly enforced. If you can switch this person from a **Can/Won't** to a **Can/Will**, then you may have the best change champion you could ask for.

The last category is **Can't/Won't**. This person needs counselling to help them understand their position and extensive "on-the-floor" support. If they do not show signs of moving to **Can/Won't** or **Will/Can't** then they are probably not suited to that role. The maxim is—if you can't change the people, change the people. Unfortunately this is sometimes required.

The typical progression between categories is shown below:

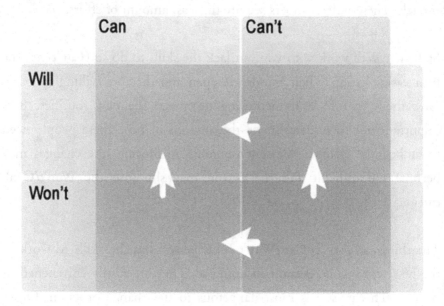

It can be said that the only time change is real is when it is at the level of the individual. Concepts such as "organisational change" or "business transformation" are valid phrases and have specific meaning. But they can also be misleading. Businesses don't actually exist. They are legal constructs. What exists are the elements of the business—the people/ plant/machinery/money etc.

To change a business means that you need to change the relationships between the elements. "People" refers to the staff members and this means actual change takes place at the individual level.

In closing I come back to the two dimensions of a change program:

1. **Engage the hearts and minds of all stakeholders.** Use this dimension to address the **Will/Won't** aspect. Get the staff to a mind-set of **Will**.

2. **Change the behaviour of the individual.** Use this dimension to address the **Can/Can't** aspect.